Martin Morris

Transatlantic Traits

Essays

Martin Morris

Transatlantic Traits
Essays

ISBN/EAN: 9783744724999

Printed in Europe, USA, Canada, Australia, Japan

Cover: Foto ©Thomas Meinert / pixelio.de

More available books at **www.hansebooks.com**

TRANSATLANTIC TRAITS.

𝔈𝔰𝔰𝔞𝔶𝔰

BY

THE HON. MARTIN MORRIS.

LONDON:
ELLIOT STOCK, 62, PATERNOSTER ROW, E.C.
1897.

To

THE HONOURABLE

WILLIAM PEEL

THIS LITTLE MEMORIAL OF OUR TRIP TO AMERICA

IS INSCRIBED.

NOTE.

'AT SEA' and 'American Traits' originally appeared in the *Nineteenth Century* and the *New Review* respectively, and I have to thank Mr. Knowles and Mr. Henley for their kind permission to republish them. They have, however, been revised and considerably enlarged for publication in their present form. The rest of the contents have not been hitherto published.

M. M.

SPIDDAL, CO. GALWAY,
September, 1897.

CONTENTS.

	PAGE
FOREWORD	1
AT SEA	7
ON TRAITS IN GENERAL	37
AMERICAN TRAITS	69
AFTWORD	123

FOREWORD.

'Keep not standing fixed and rooted,
  Briskly venture, briskly roam;
Head and hand, where'er thou foot it,
  And stout heart are still at home.

'In what land the sun does visit,
  Brisk are we, whate'er betide:
To give space for wandering is it
  That the world was made so wide.'

GOETHE.

FOREWORD.

THERE is a story that on one occasion, when an English contractor was hiring some labourers, a candidate for employment who hailed from the West of Ireland, having noticed that all his countrymen on declaring their nationality were ignominiously passed over, when asked in his turn where he came from, answered, 'Connaught;' and when further questioned as to where that was, replied, 'Beyant Ireland!' and was accordingly engaged.

This geographical exaggeration describes fairly accurately where my own home is situated, on the extreme western coast of Ireland, in the next parish, as they say, to New York—at least, with nothing intervening but the Atlantic Ocean. And how often, as I strolled

$$\pi\alpha\rho\grave{\alpha}\ \theta\tilde{\iota}\nu\alpha\ \pi o\lambda\upsilon\phi\lambda o\acute{\iota}\sigma\beta o\iota o\ \theta\alpha\lambda\acute{\alpha}\sigma\sigma\eta\varsigma,$$

have I not gazed with longing eyes out afar over the boundless waste of this mighty sea, searching in vain, like our fathers of old, for the enchanted island of the blessed, the Tir-nan-Ogue of fable and tradition! And how often, as the day slowly vanished and all around the vast horizon were cast, in superb profusion, the loveliest shades and rays of colour and light, rapt in a halo of divine love have I not fondly fancied that I descried its delicate, golden outlines in the magic splendour of our ocean sunsets! For, in very truth, is not each glorious sunset an ever-fresh Utopia, full of hope and promise, alluring and inviting us all out to a new life and home beyond?

How often, too, have I not seen some lonely peasant mount a headland cliff and wistfully strain his eyes across the 'old sea,' as he ponders in silence and sadness on the unknown fortunes of his emigrant children! For America is, and has been for many years, the Tir-nan-Ogue of the Irish peasantry, though one realized in a more tangible and sordid way than even their unenlightened imagination would picture an 'earthly paradise,' since, however ignorant they may be, they are seldom gross or material in their ideas. On the contrary, a fault, if it is one, lies in the fact that their grasp even of this world's affairs is too visionary and unpractical. Their view of life is, indeed, strangely spiritual and mystical. Considering in how niggardly and precarious a manner the bare necessities of existence have been given to them, they are heroically indifferent to material results and prospects, so that America is, truly, a rather vulgar realization of their romantic wishes and expectations.

Foreword

To an Irishman, therefore, the United States will always have a special interest and attraction. He cannot but be affected by the number of his countrymen — unmistakably Irish in word and phrase and thought and act—whom he will meet there at every turn. Indeed, in my dreams on the past and present of my unfortunate country, America seemed to rise before me like some 'Greater Ireland,' richer and happier in the future; and I would find a certain comfort in thinking over and repeating to myself those sympathetic lines of Walt Whitman on the old and new homes of the Irish race :

' Far hence amid an isle of wondrous beauty,
Crouching over a grave an ancient sorrowful mother,
Once a queen, now lean and tatter'd, seated on the ground,
Her old white hair drooping dishevel'd round her shoulders,
At her feet fallen an unused royal harp,
Long silent, she too long silent, mourning her shrouded hope and heir ;
Of all the earth her heart most full of sorrow because most full of love.
Yet a word, ancient mother,
You need crouch there no longer on the cold ground with forehead between your knees,
O you need not sit there veil'd in your old white hair so dishevel'd,
For know you the one you mourn is not in that grave.
It was an illusion, the son you love was not really dead.
The Lord is not dead, he is risen again young and strong in another country.
Even while you wept there by your fallen harp by the grave,
What you wept for was translated, pass'd from the grave,
The winds favour'd and the sea sail'd it,
And now with rosy and new blood
Moves to-day in a new country.'

There are, however, some people in the States

who think that the Irish are rather too much to the front there, and I have heard of one critic who said that America would be well rid of two nuisances if every Irishman killed a nigger and was hanged for it. But who is to blame for either? We know that the negroes did not go there of their own free will, but that, on the contrary, they were violently transported from their own homes and lashed into the country in order that they might cultivate the tobacco-plant, and thereby fill the pockets of their masters with those ill-gotten gains that have been stinking in the nostrils of men and women ever since. And, as to the immense Irish population, I would ask the Americans,—why did they send us over the potato? Because, as Edmund Burke says, 'man breeds at the mouth,' and it is therefore their own prolific root, the potato, that is to a large extent responsible for our over-population, and consequently for the necessity to emigrate.

Living, then, as I do, 'beyant Ireland'—almost within sight of Sandy Hook,—and seeing in this great continent across the water the land of promise, flowing with the milk of human kindness and the honey of universal peace and plenty for so many of my countrymen, I was very glad when a pleasant opportunity arose of visiting the United States.

AT SEA.

'Ὡς ἡδὺ τὴν θάλατταν ἄποθεν γῆς ὁρᾶν,
Ὦ μῆτερ, ἐστί, μὴ πλέοντα μηδαμῶς.
MENANDER.

'How voiceless and unfathomable are the waters on which the fragile shell of daily life reposes!'—MÆTERLINCK.

AT SEA.

I.

DOCTOR JOHNSON is reported to have said that being in a ship was like being in a gaol with the chance of being drowned; and, undoubtedly, one's 'cabined, cribbed, confined' position, even on the largest modern steamers, is a prison; but as to 'the chance of being drowned,' I was assured that on board one of the great transatlantic liners was about the safest place in the world. However, in spite of all assurances, I am inclined to think that it is generally, if not in reality, at any rate in feeling and conjecture, rather a pitch-and-toss affair. In mid-ocean, on a precipitous and moving island, in a state of constant warfare with the most powerful elements of nature, now rocked from side to side by the enormous heaves of the ocean swell, and now breathlessly buffeting the thunderous beats of wave and wind, we must feel, even under the most favourable circumstances, that we are tiding over a time of considerable danger and risk. And, accordingly, whether with or without good cause, I certainly found that an atmosphere of very great timidity and precaution permeated the whole ship.

We see, also, that we are weathering the rough assaults of forces, which, though equally inimical to all, are yet not such as are best confronted, in case of a mishap, by a united struggle, but that, on the contrary—so strong and merciless are they—the only way of escaping from their sweeping and wholesale devastation is by single, selfish efforts—*sauve qui peut*. For we know well that collective salvation will not then be the belief or order of the day, but that the survivors will be few and far between—*rari nantes in gurgite vasto*.

It is true that in the meantime we are all in the same boat; but, in these particular surroundings, similarity of situation does not kindle much sympathy or friendliness, but tends rather to rouse feelings of special rivalry and hostility. We are, therefore, peculiarly on the defensive in our mutual relations and general conduct. In fact, it is really quite ludicrous to see how careful and suspicious we become. We are on our guard from every quarter, north, south, east, and west; for, like weathercocks, we know not when or whence an ill wind may come, blowing nobody any good. Every person and object seems labelled, 'Dangerous.' Does not each represent a possible collision and upset, or at least unpleasant disturbance? A touch, a word, a look may do it. One fears lest some injudicious remark or rash act should disarrange our machinery, or that of the vessel, and perhaps spring a leak somewhere. Like the notable pots that were fellow-travellers down a stream, it is all right so long only as we take care not to crack one another. So, we move gingerly; we look askance; we speak disjointedly. Our sounds are signals; our movements balances; our seats anchorages. Nobody is at ease. Everything is angular and awkward, and liable at any moment to fall or slide away abruptly and irretrievably.

In shape and movement and mechanism the restless ship seemed to me like some monstrous shuttle, ever beating monotonous time and action, and withal weaving no tangible web in the filmy loom of the sea.

I don't mind the whole world going round, but I do rather dislike this slushy, slipshod predicament, where there is, in truth, many a slip 'twixt the cup and the lip, and many a fall between two stools. Tossed as in a churn, no one can sit still for a minute; for our poor little world is sadly out of plumb, and its levels are constantly varying and its lines crossing. We are, indeed, the whole time perilously bordering on an upsidedown state of affairs. No ground is safe—confidence is impossible. We never know where we are, or how long we may be there; and, as the fever-stricken vessel, whose clinging parasites we are, turns madly from side to side, we grow almost delirious. For the ocean is really far too susceptible of every breath of wind that may chance to pass over it; and, on account of this servile submission to *aura popularis*, we are driven, in spite of our valiant efforts to preserve a decent balance and an upright behaviour, into many an uncomfortable corner and impossible position.

Each passenger, therefore, at once adopts an attitude of extreme personal vigilance and reserve in manner and speech, and is as isolated on board the ship as the ship herself is on the ocean. To all appearances they are mere colourless bundles of human ballast. Their expressions are as blank as mummies', and their words and actions as frigid and congealed as the frozen mutton below. Not a pore is open that can be shut. Weather-proof and watertight, all their interests and desires are centred in themselves. Each man has curled himself up in his own little shell, as snugly as he can. As with the boatswain in 'The Tempest'—there is none aboard that he more loves than himself. Egotism reigns supreme. Dante's 'Inferno' is not more individual.

Thus the boat is peopled with these little human skiffs, separated and estranged from one another through a strong sense and appreciation of the general risk and jeopardy of the situation, and of the imminent possibility, at any moment, of active rivalry and antagonism; and thus, in coats of mail, as it were, we breast

At Sea

the dangers and annoyances of life at sea, and such are the prevailing considerations and influences that regulate our conduct and sentiments; and of some such sort also is man, I fear, when placed between the devil and the deep sea. To tell the truth and shame the last-mentioned gentleman, the fact is that we are only too glad and thankful to be left thus high and dry, both by the receding waves and by our retiring companions, and in neither case would we invite more intimate relations.

This nervous spirit dominating everything, and our defensive manner and unfriendly aspect, are by no means attractive. In fact, on board a ship is not, for many reasons, a pleasant or sociable place, and most passengers are very near land again before they consent to become even nodding acquaintances. Such close quarters — on deck and at table, sharing state-rooms and cabins and saloons — seem like an attempt to enforce a companionship, which in itself most people dislike and resent; and so, if only for this reason, we are as cool and distant as it is possible to be in so limited an area, until we have had time to recover somewhat from the shock of this inevitable and ubiquitous proximity. It is, certainly, no place for a recluse, who ought either to stay at home, or, if he goes to sea, be able at least to paddle his own canoe.

Nor is this climatic pillory becoming to the physical, or the sartorial sides of our nature.

Saturated on deck with the salt sweat of the brine and unstinted fresh air, or pent up in airtight holes for hours or perhaps days, our physical appearance is in neither case at its best, while the costumes worn, especially the ladies' marine garments, are extremely ugly. So we are not, taken altogether, a pretty kettle of fish—or, rather, we are. Indeed, a collection of passengers at sea looks uncommonly like a great cargo of human rubbish, gathered from all parts of the globe, and heaped together into one discordant load for the express purpose of being carted out into midocean and there ignominiously consigned to the waves and deeps of oblivion. If, however, it should be lucky enough to escape this appropriate and timely end, and thus, as it were, reprieved, should manage to reach in safety a landing-stage, there is some justification for this merciful prolongation of life to be found in the remarkable transformation scene that takes place when the happy hour of release approaches. Grace and chivalry once more relate the sexes; there is an extraordinary change for the better in their physical appearance; colour and expression again declare themselves, and hair falls into place and form, while their figures and limbs seem actually to take a new shape as they stand once more on steady ground and, with autochthonic pride and stateliness, tread in the old familiar footsteps of terrestrial life; and clothes become again decorative.

Verily to disembark is to escape as from a gaol, and the minute the 'unplumbed, salt, estranging' gulf that cuts us off from home and hearth is bridged by the gangway, pushing forward, bag and baggage, we hasten across to much-coveted freedom and exercise of mind and body, to roam and to stretch to our hearts' and legs' content after our long, cramped confinement. Without delay we settle down on the soft lap of luxurious Earth, and, shaking the spray off the hem of our garments, we would, in our great joy and delight —like dogs, like donkeys, like anything—roll and roll in the dust and the grass. For physical, and moral, and intellectual, as well as æsthetic, reasons, a landscape is a necessary background to the human figure.

II.

Anyone who has ever been on a long sea voyage knows its little excitements and diversifications—the reading of the log-book, which is the daily newspaper, the standard concert, the drawing of sweepstakes, etc. It is not lively. There is nothing especially entertaining or dramatic in a sponge-bag, and such-like is our *milieu* for the time being. But any life or fun there was seemed to me to be among the steerage passengers. There humour and pathos, love and laughter, accidents and tragedies, might be seen. Yet, curiously enough, a great part of their time was passed in religious exercises—singing, and preaching, and praying. Some were apprehensive and in earnest, some indifferently acquiesced, and some evidently found it an amusing pastime. One young man, with a damsel leaning on each arm and followed by a procession, paraded about singing snatches of hymns in a very convivialist, if not revivalist fashion. But, beyond such mild efforts, the voyage was quite uneventful. We fell in with no strange islands or slumbering monsters, and we saw no sea-serpents. Such superstitions of the ocean seem of late to have subsided largely, or, perhaps, the mythical is not much in my line. Neither was the unusual commonplace. There were no deaths, nor were there any births, as there often are, and, although there may have been some betrothals unknown to me, there were no marriages. And nobody fell overboard.

I am not an ancient mariner. This was, in fact, my first really outlandish expedition, and I must say I found it gratified, with one possible exception, none of the ordinary pleasures and tastes of life. In the first place, even the best ship can scarcely be considered a cosy or comfortable abode. Like some huge lavatory, it has everywhere a hard, cold, petrified aspect, and I thought my narrow berth, or shelf, preferable only to the rather too wide bed of the ocean outside. On land the wind may on exceptional occasions make our homes tremble to their very foundations, but here with tiring tremor, or perhaps more barefaced action, it unceasingly tosses the billows of the sea and the pillows of one's couch, to our indescribable confusion and dismay; and no one can find a spot whereon to lay his head in peace. Then the food tastes insipid and artificial. Meat kept in ice seems as though it had been washed and rinsed until all the essence was gone, while of course it is not the first time that the fish has been at sea. There is no delicious flavour of clay in the vegetables, and the water one drinks has come from no fresh mountain spring.

But it is the home and paradise of the idle and lazy. On the sea one has no use for feet or legs at all, since the ship herself does all the motion, although she even, as in the Irish song, 'walks through the water without any feet.' One cannot stand or walk or run except on a few short planks; there are no 'fresh woods or pastures new' to turn to. The unwebbed toes and the unfledged arms of the human kind are thoroughly useless and out of place. Man is, in truth, every bit as bad on the water as a fish is on dry ground. He is an exotic. He is most distinctly not in his element. The 'biped without feathers' looks, indeed, pitiably naked and foolish in these cold, unsheltered regions, where only a mermaid or a Dagon, with their piscine tails, could possibly enjoy themselves. There is, therefore, nowhere to go, nor is there anything to do. Nor, once the ship has started, is any escape or return possible. As with a letter thrown into the pillar-box, there is now an irreparable finality about one's plight and fortune.

Living on board a ship, a man has, in fact, no alternative before him but to drown. At last we have got time to spare, but now man's whole business and occupation, as an intelligent child of earth, has come to an untimely end. One does not read or write much, and people are not conversational at sea, and any talk there may be is but far-fetched reminiscences of distant climes and forgotten interests. Time hangs heavily on one's hands, and one is content, and even glad, to join in any foolish game or sport to help to while it away.

Why, one cannot even think! This vast void of wind and water almost takes away the breath and sustenance of life, suffocating and annihilating the powers of the mind and body. Man's physical properties and cares, at all times a trouble and danger to the welfare of the soul, are simply ruinous to it on the ocean. It is, indeed, quite awful to contemplate how sterile and dull we would become if long at sea. The infinite volume of the ocean would, I fear, mentally drown us, for such interminableness and monotony do not at all conduce to intellectual fruition. Eternity is, I suspect, thoughtless. Philosophy in the clouds can only be true very metaphorically, for I cannot believe that any train of reason or system of thought was ever worked out in a ship or a balloon. In fact, none but a man of straw can hope to cross successfully this treacherous waste. No matter of weight and solidity will receive from it even superficial support. The sailor skims through life; his views are skin-deep. After all, it is only in the study, or at any rate in the fields, that the human brain can flourish and be productive. But, voyaging in this boundless and empty space, where only clouds and rain are made, there is nothing whatever to catch the wandering eye or to fix and occupy the vacant mind. There are no objects, no distinctions, no limits, no standards, no contrasts. Nothing rises or falls, or appears and vanishes—for the ocean has long ago found its dull, unchanging level. Day and night, even, are much the same, since there is nothing for the sun to disclose or for darkness to hide. And such blank, spacious vision, where nothing meets the eye, brings about absolute mental and physical blindness; for are not visual interruption and concentration of the mind the actual causes of all sight and thought? To select or discriminate, therefore, is impossible. Who knows one wave from another? Who can pin the ever-shifting cloud? What ray of thought can pierce pure atmosphere? Can man cope with the inane?

Thus are we blindly swimming in a sea of unbroken liquid, and the solids of life, so to speak, have been left far behind; it is indeed a soupy, sloppy fare, tasteless and unpalatable to the mental appetite of man. 'Praised be our Lord for my sister, the water, who is very serviceable to us, and humble and precious and clear,' cried the poet of Assisi; but he was thinking of the fresh moisture of his native hills—the pure streams and gentle lakes, the bubbling well-springs and the dew upon the grass—and, if I may say so *cum grano salis*, there is all the difference in the world.

Thus sundered from the body of life, we reel and we grope and we gasp, and flounder hopelessly in our frantic efforts to find any help or support. In vain we look, amid the scene of universal deluge about us, for some fixed point to cling to and find a refuge in, but no hospitable port or friendly light greets us in mid-ocean. Unkind Earth has, in fact, given us the cold shoulder. Like Archimedes, we, also, are in want of room to stand on in order to set to at our work; for at sea there is no *locus standi* for any human being. Man is in every way out of his depth; whatever giants of old could do, the pigmy of to-day cannot wade very far, while he would require more than modern faith to find a safe footing on so sceptical a foundation. So, his hopes are uncertain; his views undefined; his reflections unfathomable; and life but a speculative flotation.

The products of the mind are as barren and unstable as the bubbles rising and bursting in the surf; neither can escape into separate and substantial existence. *Ex nihilo nihil.* All is vanity. A mental vacancy appears, indeed, to pervade and colour the whole of this wishy-washy realm of the finny tribe, of whom the complaint has with justice been made, that it is impossible to obtain from them a single instructive look or sound—

with the one exception of that miraculous occasion on which they are said to have listened attentively to the eloquent words of a saint. A spiritual chill seems to come over us in their domain, as though we, also, were cold-blooded animals. We, too, grow deaf and dumb in this voiceless world, for, as you know, ' the things that live in the sea are all mute.' Our thoughts and feelings become dormant. Sight, hearing, taste, touch, and smell—all are painfully circumscribed and benumbed. It is like some uncanny, hibernating season of the fertile mind and warm body of man. A flatulent stagnancy oppresses and overpowers us, and, with one last gurgling murmur, we succumb to the degraded level of jelly-fish.

And how wretched and feeble is this blunt, comatose condition of the senses beside the vigorous health and strength of true manhood! And how hateful and ruinous is this torpid, ichthyoidal existence to the earnest soul and consciousness of man, who, in order to flourish and bear fruit, like a flower of the field, must be firmly planted and rooted. For he cannot, like some plants of seaweed whose roots even float upon the surface of the sea, live and thrive while thus drifting before the wind. He cannot, like the halcyon, build his nest upon the water. He is rather a bird of passage, who finds here no home or resting-place. Unhappy man, whose supreme distinction, as man, consists in being able to rise above Nature and get the better of his tyrannous environment! But here, bound hand and foot by his unnatural surroundings, his special prerogative is completely lost, and he is forced to abdicate his crowning faculties—the intellect and soul—and, like one of the lowest animals, to accept without question or debate his dull, insensate existence. Man is not man or master of his fate.

It is a precarious existence, too—just keeping our heads above water. For we are but puppets, bobbing for very life in the storm and stress of the ocean, on the secret brow of which, even when at rest, dreaded doom treacherously broods. The smooth desert of the ocean, ἀκύμων νηνέμοις, is too ominous of the calm that precedes a storm to be called peaceful. The sleep of the sea is that of a sleeping wolf, and we never know when we may not be fleeing for our lives before the ravenous waves in our track. There is, it always seems to me, some awful iron hand underneath its softest velvet covering. Extremely sensitive to touch—on the slightest provocation radiating in ever-widening circles of intelligence—it is equally bold to strike. Tragic uncertainty, therefore, in its most unrelenting form, reigns throughout these unfamiliar regions, and it was not without reason that long sea-voyages were of old considered sacrilegious, as tempting Fate too much. So, we are all fatalists at sea, just as those who live by the shore generally are; and mere human character and will are completely submerged in the mysterious

At Sea

depths of destiny and chance. Man is, in fact, no longer a free agent in mind or body, but the hapless victim of strange unearthly powers.

> 'Unfathomable Sea! whose waves are years,
> Ocean of Time, whose waters of deep woe
> Are brackish with the salt of human tears!
> Thou shoreless flood, which in thy ebb and flow
> Claspest the limits of mortality!
> And sick of prey, yet howling on for more,
> Vomitest thy wrecks on its inhospitable shore,
> Treacherous in calm, and terrible in storm!
>   Who shall put forth on thee,
>   Unfathomable Sea?'

It is, indeed, difficult to remember that we are as near heaven by sea as by land.

And how impersonal we must and do become! Dipped, as it were, in the waters of Lethe, we have entirely shaken off all our usual manners and morals and customs as obsolete remnants of some antediluvian order of things. We have grown unworldly enough to please anyone. All old associations—local, national, legal, of birth, name, home, class, country, of kinship and friendship — evaporate in this realm of nothingness. Variations of age, sex, character, of religion, habits, pursuits, means, have no room or opportunity for display. Passion and purpose have no vent. There is nothing to covet or to be jealous or angry or greedy about. All social duties and rights have been swamped in a wild, anarchical abyss of antinomian spaciousness. The whole ship and crew seemed to me like some poor, banished bit of existence, where, clustered together in mean attire and pitiable want, the exposed foundlings and exiled scapegoats of mankind passed their miserable, empty lives, far from all distinction and civilization. For we had, indeed, drained the bitter cup of misfortune, and, like the famous crew turned into swine, we, too, bereft of speech and hideously changed in form and feeling, could but bewail our lost humanity.

Thus, wiped off the face of the earth, we are lost in the splash and the mist, and one's soul becomes as dreary and desolate as that of the man in the moon, and one's very existence almost as mythological. For we are now skirting along no neighbouring coast, hostile or friendly; we are within the pale of no nation's waters, but are out on the high seas—disowned and disinherited—like so much discarded flotsam. The size of the sea is its solitude. And looking across the pathless desert before one—far away ' unto the confines of light and darkness '—how deep and cold seems the awful infinitude of this unearthly pelagic sphere, whose swamping sway extends over two-thirds of the globe! All around one vast, trembling, threatening plain, beneath which nameless monsters in hidden silence live; above us, endless shades of shivering gray and blue. Ah, would that one could fill the cruel gulf that separates land from land and man from man, making lonely islands of all our thoughts and hopes and loves!

Sea and sky; billows and breezes; light without sweetness; sight without objects; freedom in space; life in a world without love; one wash of blue and gray—it is truly a vain and vague existence, floating in this nebulous world of froth and vapour. And within such fluid and aerial envelopments—since all things then seem very cognate and interchangeable—we are well able to realize how the whole of Nature is perhaps one and the same stuff, how ether may be only a more rarefied form of matter permeating even the solid structure of crystals, and matter only a more compressed form of ether, or both of them but forms of energy. In a long-continued storm is it not actually true that the limits and distinction of the sea, 'mounting to the welkin's cheek,' are completely annihilated—'the heaven all spray and the ocean all cloud'? But, although there may be this natural affinity, there are no feelings of human kinship or familiarity in the scene, for the sea and the sky are most distant from, and foreign to our physical organism. Human beings are as fit for life at sea as a crab is for flying. At one time of his development man may have been no more than an animal, but, as far as I can by hints and possible inclinations in myself revive his earliest aboriginal habits and instincts, he was never either a fish or a bird. Yet scientists tell us that at one time there was nothing but water-life in the world, and that land animals are comparatively late inventions, and, as evidence of this, they point to the snail wandering over the earth with his sea-shell still on his back, and they will also explain how a worm one day crept up a tree, and how it had to grow wings in order to get down again. But all this, if ever, was a long time ago, and I, for my part, found this atmosphere of wind and wave so strange and uncongenial that I doubt very much if my ancestors were at any stage of their gradual evolution able to swim or to fly, although perhaps they may once have been able to crawl and to climb. Lucretius is perfectly right: men do not spring from the sea, nor herds, and other cattle, burst from the sky.

It seems, indeed, clear to me that we human beings are essentially landlubbers, and that we must stick, like leeches, to earth for our very lifeblood. Is it not a fact, that, when life begins to fail, our senses swim and our wits vanish into the air? Is not death a sort of unpleasant drunkenness, a fatal inundation as it were, by which the equipoise that sustains life is clouded and upset? Whatever may be Nature's feelings in the matter, may we not say that man certainly abhors a vacuum?

And in this vapid sphere of water and air, how ardently one longs for a good handful of dry, brown clay! How one's feet itch for the sure and safe touch of soil! How divine Earth now seems to us! On the dead, barren boards of the deck one thinks of her as teeming and sprouting with rich, luxuriant life. A particle of dust, even, is now a sacred and treasured relic of past terrestrial bliss, and as for a blade of grass or a sprig of green foliage, they would be as manna from heaven to one's famished senses and orphaned soul. Verily Earth is our mother. In these ethereal regions, hemmed in by the ocean on all sides, I must confess that I found myself to be a gross, unabashed materialist, and shamelessly wished to be, as they say, 'immersed in matter.' Why, the poor vessel herself is not, I do believe, too happy —thus far from all harbours and moorings. Have you, at least, never noticed, at the pier or by the wharf, how lovingly she leans upon the land, rubbing herself against it just as a dog does against his master's leg?

And how deeply pathetic it was to watch the antics of these exiled children of Earth as, by diligently pacing up and down the deck, with much turning and twisting they endeavoured, like hares, to cover many miles in a small ambit, and, by stamping noisily on the boards, vainly and foolishly tried to recall the joys of terra firma and the voluptuous delights of a long, unbroken walk! For no amount of treading and tramping will draw from the hard, cold, close-shaven, and well-scrubbed boards of a ship's deck a vestige of Earth's soft touch and fond caressing warmth,— what the poet refers to when he says:

'The press of my foot to the earth springs a hundred affections;'

and the futile attempt to do so only reminded me of a tame sparrow I once saw that used to flap its wings and try to douse itself in the polished, glossy surface of a mahogany table.

How wanting, too, in local interest and colour of its own the whole scene before one is! For in mid-ocean there is none of the music and beauty of the sea. It is on the shore that the waves break into resounding speech and song, and the sweet tattle of the tide entertains one. By the cliffs and the rocks, among the shells and pebbles on the beach, it is that the sea finds its human voice, and that all the romance and poetry of its life take place. How many hours have I not spent there, watching the sea as it played in lively dalliance with the unforthcoming land, ever and anon approaching and retreating, like a baffled but persevering lover, with many a furtive kiss, and with how many a smart slap in the face, too! But out here there is no tide or current of any sort; no ebb or flow is perceptible—none of the come and go of love and life. It is an unvaried scene, without feature or expression—gray, dull, obvious, endless, tiresome, deadly. This cold, passionless, sexless world should be, once and for all, judicially declared null and void—and I do so.

Thoreau found it employment enough to watch the progress of the seasons at Walden, but he could not have so occupied himself at sea. For, unlike the rest of Nature, the ocean has no seasons—no spring, or summer, or autumn, or winter; no fresh life and growth, no new scents, no birth or death. It has been well called evergreen. Snow even does not cover or affect it; while after rain the ship seems the only wet place. If all the plants that grow on the Earth are language to her many thoughts and fancies, what a bald and barren numskull is the ocean, with never a thought or a tree! Nor can time imprint any tale or tidings on its fluctuating surface. The past leaves no traces. It has no records or history. Unlike crumbling ruins, wrecks are quickly swallowed up and all vestiges obliterated; a house built on sand lasts longer. For the ocean has no memory. The fields of Marathon and Waterloo outlive Salamis and Trafalgar. For all I know there may be whole cities under the sea, for are there not legends that tell of bells heard pealing on calm and still days, and of spires seen in the hollow of the waves when the sea is rough? But, as a rule, all submarine stories and experiences are buried far too deep for even the most adventurous diver or Wet-as-weed. 'What an imagination God has!' was Tennyson heard to say, as once in his college-days he looked deeply and earnestly into the subaqueous life of a stream near Cambridge. But who has seen the 'untrampled floor' of the sea? Who could sound the ocean *au fond*? Unless, perhaps, the imagination of the great poet, thus:

> 'Methought I saw a thousand fearful wrecks;
> A thousand men that fishes gnaw'd upon;
> Wedges of gold, great anchors, heaps of pearl,
> Inestimable stones, unvalued jewels,

All scatter'd in the bottom of the sea.
Some lay in dead men's skulls; and in those holes
Where eyes did once inhabit, there were crept,
As 'twere in scorn of eyes, reflecting gems,
That woo'd the slimy bottom of the deep,
And mock'd the dead bones that lay scatter'd by.'

Or thus:

'The world below the brine,
  Forests at the bottom of the sea, the branches and leaves,
  Sea-lettuce, vast lichens, strange flowers and seeds, the thick tangle, openings, and pink turf,
  Different colours—pale gray and green, purple, white, and gold—the play of light through the water;
  Dumb swimmers there among the rocks, coral, gluten, grass, rushes, and the aliment of the swimmers;
  Sluggish existences grazing there suspended, or slowly crawling close to the bottom;
  The sperm-whale at the surface blowing air and spray, or disporting with his flukes;
  The leaden-eyed shark, the walrus, the turtle, the hairy sea-leopard, and the sting-ray;
  Passions there, war, pursuits, tribes, sight in those ocean-depths, breathing that thick-breathing air, as so many do.
  The change thence to the sight here, and to the subtle air breathed by beings like us who walk this sphere;
  The change onward from ours to that of beings who walk other spheres.'

Oh, this great unimpressionable power! And the littleness and futility of man on the waves! For, as you will remember, a broomstick has been proved to be quite as useless and absurd against the ocean as a fork with Nature! Or what, in all seriousness, can we hope or attempt to do or to see where even the hand of the Creator is not visible or present? For is not this the material, 'without form and void,' which the Divine Sculptor left untouched on the day in that memorable week when He made ' the dry land appear'? It may be difficult to see the trees for the wood, but who can see anything for the overwhelming ocean? Can we even see it? I have heard that Cortez 'stared' at the Pacific, but I have wondered much how he managed to do it, and agree rather with Charles Lamb, who complained that he had never seen the ocean, but only an insignificant bit of it. Did not even the great Newton say that he seemed to have been all his life gathering a few shells on the shore, whilst a boundless ocean of truth lay beyond and unknown to him? The very progress of the ship through its multitudinous waves is impossible to detect and difficult to believe in, and at the journey's end the land comes on one as a surprise; and I, for my part, would not have been much astonished if, like some ill-starred windfall, we had never reached our destination. For in this gigantic whirlpool—of ceaseless motion without any changing, though with a great deal of chopping —there are no landmarks or signposts, to say nothing of milestones. Nor are there any stations to reach or resting-stages to stop at. We never change horses—perhaps wisely, since this is said to be inadvisable in the middle even of a stream. And, accordingly, I never really felt that we were getting over any ground or approaching any end, but, for all I could see or understand, we were moving round and round in a circle, which, had it not been for the compass—the sailor's cross of salvation—we might, I suppose, still be doing.

Thus wayward and undefined and irreducible to ordinary sense and intelligence seemed to me the whole of our course in this mutable world; and serious thoughts on round, unreturning life itself arose in my mind.

III.

Thus, cooped up like hens in the middle of a great pool, the time passes away in slumber and vacuity—in much feeding and roosting and a certain amount of discontented croaking and picking.

But there are times in this rather squalid existence when the soul can emerge and rise to the purest heights of spiritual triumph and enjoyment; rare moments, when the true purposes of life become evident and conscious realities, and the soul, touched with emotion, breathes eternal loyalty to its high possibilities; hours spent by day in sea-dreaming, and by night in stargazing; calm days, when all above is a dome of light and the waters around one smooth resplendent flood; clear nights, when the sea 'bares her bosom to the moon,' whose bright shadow, soft and evanescent like a golden rainbow, lights and adorns her deep, dark rest; stirring, dashing times, when the width and the freedom and the wildness of the scene rouse and exhilarate the strong, rebellious spirit in one; fickle moods, when the perpetual change and motion of this fleeting world delight one; lovely, chaste mornings, when the electric purity and freshness of the sea and the air enchant one; long, sultry afternoons, passed in drowsily listening to the constant, hissing splash as we crush and cross the waves, and break into a foaming wound the livid hue of the water,—for the blood of the sea is white; gorgeous, fiery evenings, when the blaze of the setting sun and the glow of the spreading ocean vie with one another in surpassing magnificence of glory and promise. And how often, drifting thus between two oceans, one infinite arching overhead, and one fathomless sweeping underneath, the vast space of the sky with its countless stars above, and the unknown depths of the sea with its myriad waves below, alone, in the solemn stillness of 'the huge and thoughtful night,' and bathed in the everlasting mystery of life and death, would I wistfully look up into the deep vault of the veiled heavens, and again peer down into the dark hollow of the hidden waters!

> 'Stars silent rest o'er us;
> Graves under us silent.'

It was strange and startling, indeed, to think of this little oasis of life and humanity in the wide wilderness of the desert-ocean. For I found the Atlantic very uninhabited, except by fish, and they were mostly beneath our notice. We seldom sighted a passing ship, and only occasionally saw the backs of plunging dolphins or the foam-fountains of the 'sea-shouldering' whale. Birds alone were our constant attendants and companions.

But I must not fail to mention how, one beautiful clear afternoon, four magnificent icebergs came floating by. Their dazzling lustre in the bright sunshine, glowingly reflected in the watery mirror around, was superb; and as the ship passed close by them, one after the other in procession, they seemed to me like great ocean swans that had strayed from their northern nests and were now aimlessly swimming about this shoreless pond in search of home and rest—some with their stately necks reared high above the luminous water in crystal glory, some with their heads gracefully buried, in arctic repose, in the fluffy, snow-white plumage of their softly-folded wings. And, as the sun's rays fell upon them and the seabreezes blew around them, they sparkled all over in shimmering sprays of silvery radiance, their fern-like feathers of frost and foam were gently turned and ruffled, and the sheen of the encircling blue broke against their emerald-hued sides into a thousand rippling waves of motion and light—one star-quivering, sun-flashing, sea-glittering scene of glacial splendour. And, again, as we slowly left them far behind us, I fancied them to be the loveliest of sea-lilies, cruelly torn from their white bed in the north and wafted down the world's great gulf-stream; and, as they listlessly floated towards warmer climes, little by little fading and melting away into its absorbing depths, —pure water-blossoms, dissolving pearls of snow.

These phantoms of the ocean looked so peaceful and innocent that it was difficult to regard them as one of the greatest dangers of the voyage, which in foggy weather they are, although there is, I believe, some slight chance of seeing them in time, owing to their brilliant whiteness and towering height. Apart, however, from the mere danger, I am glad that we escaped a collision, since, in such a catastrophe, though doubtless the unholy part of my nature would have been inclined to curse this 'harmless albatross,' all my poetic sympathies would have been on the side of so fair and fascinating an opponent. For, in spite of the ship's orthodox gender — she is feminine because the true sailor loves her — I imagined her to be a mighty, screw-driving, smoke-belching, vulcan-like blacksmith (I had but lately been inspecting the many gigantic furnaces and instruments of force that propel her), with club-feeted, halting blades forging his iron way and will in a brutal attempt to assault the cool, fresh, morning purity of some spotless goddess, born of the sea. Certainly as these icebergs, aurora-like, tremulous, and delicate, calmly glided along, our noise and motion, as, leviathan-like, with smoking nostrils and burning eyeballs, we ploughed and splashed by, seemed rude, indecent, and unpardonable.

We did not catch sight of another danger—'derelicts.' I regret this, as I should have much liked to have seen a great naked-ribbed vessel, adrift and unmanned and deserted by every living creature, its skeleton hulk still lying unburied on this fluid field of storm-fighting.

But we did have a view of the greatest 'derelict' of all, in my opinion, between England and America. For I shall not soon forget how, as the first morning broke after leaving Liverpool, we found ourselves anchored in the beautiful harbour of Queenstown, with its picturesquely-situated Cathedral on the brow of the terraced declivity on which the little town is built. This lovely glimpse of Ireland was especially dear and touching to me, since, meeting thus at sea, it seemed as though my native land had actually come out a part of the way on purpose to see me off and bid me a 'God-speed'; and well may I say, when, with the hearty good wishes of those on shore, we started on our voyage across the ocean,

> 'The ship was cheered, the harbour cleared,
> Merrily did we drop
> Below the kirk, below the hill,
> Below the lighthouse top.'

And long shall I remember, also, as through the whole of that afternoon we receded further and further from the fading land, sadly gazing back at its dim and distant edge on the far horizon; and how, as I thought of the Old World that we were leaving behind, and of the New World that we were hurrying to, it seemed like the faint, thin tinge and outline of an old waning moon, pale and dying, yet clearly visible; and so it remained in my eyes even after, continuing our globular course, we had come round on the first crescent of the rich, new, waxing moon.

ON TRAITS IN GENERAL.

'It is not worth while to go round the world in order to count the cats in Zanzibar.'—THOREAU.

'There is a way of killing truth by truths. Under the pretence that we want to study it more in detail, we pulverize the statue.'—AMIEL.

ON TRAITS IN GENERAL.

I.

A TRUE national type is an imaginary figure incorporating the many real qualities or traits that lie scattered throughout a country or people; and just as the Apollo Belvedere is an expression of male beauty, and not a copy of some particular man, or the Venus of Milo is as like a black woman as a white one, so this national type is fully represented by no one person, although contributed to by nearly all to some extent. There ought, therefore, to be no attempt to confine to a particular example, or to compare with some known instance, anything that may be said in the course of an endeavour to point out some of the traits that go to form such a type. And if there should be, the exaggeration of the remark would probably seem very gross. For in essays of this kind, where it is the writer's express wish and intention to impart general ideas only, and not to supply information of actual facts, each thought and saying should have all the size and strength and emphasis of a wide generalization, based on innumerable examples, suggestions, and inferences; and accordingly it would not be reasonable or fair to submit them to the narrow test of concrete verification. Traits of national life and character cannot be accurately gauged and adjusted, as though they were just so much statistical stuffing. A true type is, in fact, often avowedly false to the reality, if by that is meant some specific instance; but it should always be true to the spirit, or the universal and essential in any instance.

Neither do these 'American traits' that follow include in their survey the exceptional or individual. They do not purport to deal with all the vagaries of whim and fancy and caprice, or with any of the singularities due to special class or culture; and where these are very remarkable, it must be peculiarly difficult to form any idea of the typical. However, this is not the case in America, where the variations in personal qualities are few and slight, and where the similarities are decided and unfailing. For, though American life presents a clear and effective image to the mind, this is not so much because of its strikingness in any respect as on account of its widespread monotony. The picturesque does not catch the eye, but constant repetition fixes the view. There is everywhere a strong family likeness in the ways and manners of the people, who, one and all, may be

On Traits in General 41

said to be very characteristic of one another. Soon, therefore—perhaps too soon—the prevalent Yankee traits become evident and unmistakable even by the casual observer.

II.

From the way in which some travellers write about the countries that they have been visiting, one would be almost led to suppose that they had actually discovered them. Unfortunately I do not think that I can pretend to have done this in the case of America, as it is really too notorious about Columbus, and accordingly, if only for this reason, I trust I shall not be found guilty of making any preposterous claims on this score. And yet I have seen this great historical axiom gravely questioned, just as it is still unknown how the aboriginal inhabitants of the continent got there, the best surmise being that it was 'a skating-party from Friesland' that first peopled the country; while some irreverently say that there was an Adam and Eve for both continents. But, however it may be with that problem, as to the other, the vulgar opinion undoubtedly is that about four centuries ago one Christopher Columbus, when searching for the back-door of Asia, came upon the front-door of America, and was the first European to do so and live to tell the tale, and I am perfectly willing to leave the matter there. It is also, I think, pretty well known that in the interval since 1492 Columbus has had many followers and I many forerunners. It is, therefore, quite plain that I came on the scene somewhat too late to put in any prior claims to a grand and original discovery of the country; and, as to the numerous accounts and stories of the people published by my predecessors, I can only say that it will be my earnest endeavour, in fairness both to them and to myself, to keep as clear as I can of them and their tracks.

With this end in view I shall, then, above all, avoid giving wordy descriptions of natural scenery and of well-known places and events, especially as it is my opinion that there is here, as in life generally, seldom any necessity or capacity to properly name or describe things, and that ordinarily our entire aim and wish should be only to see them clearly and acknowledge them, and so absorb as far as possible their spirit or meaning, their qualities and influence, for use and being in all that we say and do. So, nothing would induce me to attempt to draw a verbal picture of the falls and surroundings of Niagara; for the scene before one there is of such stupendous volume and power and depth that a long time would, I fear, elapse —perhaps the river run dry—before there would arise, even in the inspired soul of the poet, the true word, the divine utterance, that sacred speech of genius, which exists somewhere, to name and define all objects of sense and thought. As for ordinary folk, they can seldom be trusted to choose even a tolerably right word. 'That is a

On Traits in General

majestic waterfall!' observed a gentleman at the Falls of Clyde. 'Yes, sir,' replied Coleridge, delighted with the accuracy of the epithet, particularly as he had been lately settling in his own mind the precise meaning of the words, grand, majestic, sublime, etc. 'It *is*,' he repeated, 'a *majestic* waterfall!' 'Sublime and beautiful!' added his friend. I will therefore only just say this: That I would be glad to be as sure and certain of anything in life as I am that Lake Erie *falls* into Lake Ontario.

Nor shall I, however much I should like to, ask you to wander with me, at least for any length of time, beneath the historic elms of Concord village, and round by Walden pond, and so back through the beautiful cemetery of Sleepy Hollow, where lie the mortal remains of Emerson, Thoreau, and Hawthorne. It is a sad thing arriving too late to see those whom you love and admire, and to have to be content with visiting their graves; and this was my melancholy feeling as I stood on that consecrated spot and thought of these great departed spirits; and the touching lines of lament by the last surviving one of that distinguished group of men who made Boston celebrated in the middle of this century, came into my mind:

> 'The mossy marbles rest
> On the lips that he has prest
> In their bloom;
> And the names he loved to hear
> Have been carved for many a year
> On the tomb.'

The huge block of rough granite, unshaped and unhewn, that marks the grave of Emerson is a very striking and emblematic memorial of this great man. Substantial and nonconforming to any plan or system, this piece of pure natural strength and independence stands alone and self-reliant, while from all over it scintillate, like so many sparkling epigrams of wit and wisdom, a thousand brilliant forms of crystal. And, as we passed on down the wooded walks of this quiet resting-place, I felt as though I were in some remote garden—far from the world—where innocence and genius lived in peaceful seclusion and happiness. The benign spirit of Emerson seemed to smile through the mottling pine-trees above, lighting up and kindling the whole of this dead world around into life with the brightness and warmth of the sun; while the quaint thoughts of Thoreau, original and suggestive, seemed embodied in the cones of strange shape but rich seed that lay strewn along the winding path before one. And outside this garden of 'lovely and soothing death,' I knew that men only toiled and sweated.

But still less shall long, wearisome descriptions of innumerable cities and places detain me. Neither that rich centre, New York City, nor fair Boston, with its charming surroundings, nor the sylvan beauties of Philadelphia, nor the neat heights of hilly Baltimore, nor the well-planned avenues of Washington, the town of magnificent distances, nor the Capitol and the White House, nor Harvard College and Independence Hall, nor Washington's home and Franklin's grave, nor the Hudson River, nor the wide expanse of blue Ontario, nor the glory of the autumn, or fall, foliage, with its wonderful display of colour, a sample of which we have in the Virginian creeper, shall detain me. Yet all these places and sights, and many more, have left lasting impressions on my memory, and my thoughts would gladly linger around them, recalling to mind with gratitude and respect many passing friends, though in a rather confused manner, since my visits were brief and hurried.

I shall not, either, dilate on the gastronomic pleasures—or the reverse—of terrapin or canvasback, of pumpkin pies or gin cocktails, of succotash or clam-chowder. I shall give no musical dissertation on the popular refrains of 'Yankee Doodle' or 'The Bowery.' I have no collection of American anecdotes and phrases. Neither have I any statistics to furnish the inquiring mind with. I am not a good reporter, nor much of a hand at names or figures. I can give very few facts. I do not know many. Least of all have I a supply of examples and instances for everything that I say; for I have no wish to teach after the kindergarten fashion. I go so far as to flatter myself that that method is too elementary for my audience, and to say further that, in order to learn anything from me, a person must be able to appreciate broad generalizations, and to find profit and use in the abstract, symbolic interpretation of matters; for I seek principles in all life, and, in my search for them, make and re-make many theories until I think that I have satisfactorily reached them.

I do not, then, desire to write a modern anabasis, telling how many stages and parasangs we travelled each day, and the number of populous, prosperous, and great cities that we met with. You will, at all events, be spared that deadly production, the diary of a tourist, with its detailed and faithful account of all his comings and goings and doings. I must confess, too, that I cannot speak as an eyewitness of some great sight or function, for I do not remember that we happened to come just in the nick of time for anything very unusual or wonderful anywhere. I have no exciting adventures to describe or special privileges to record. I have nothing whatever exceptional to boast of. Nor, again, can I tell what is the population of Brooklyn, or how many hogs are killed daily or annually in Chicago, or what is the geological composition of the soil, or how high any of the mountains are—for I do not know these things.

I have, in fact, accurate information about, or authorities for, scarcely anything that I say. I made no inquiries. All my experiences were passive. What I received I got without asking for. So my accounts must not be audited; they must be taken *in globo;* for I would always only give the sum-total without trying to explain how it is reached. For my part, I have never

On Traits in General 47

weighed or measured or counted anything in life I leave all that to tradesmen, whether grocers or tailors, pedants or versifiers.

III.

The truth is, that in all matters of this sort I value only the general significance or effect, and if any experience or sight should seem to me to fail in this respect, I am wholly uninterested in all the facts and figures that analytical investigation or diligent study may root out, since I believe that their real significance lies ever in the actual impression that they make as wholes, and not in the recounting of the properties that they may be proved to possess. There are few things in the world that you will see better by pulverizing them. A general impression, though, like life itself, more suggestive than distinct, is, as a rule, in my opinion, truer and more valuable than the clearest and most precise enumeration of the various separate ingredients that go to form a combination, because, as a matter of fact, these were never so seen, but were always parts of an apparently indivisible whole. For instance, in my picture I could certainly represent the rain in slanting lines, as the impression is, and not in distinct, single drops, as the fact is, since it is not intended to be a scientific diagram or a chemical analysis. Such a picture, I admit, may unduly exaggerate some predominant quality, or at least greatly diminish a less significant one, according to the bearing and influence of all the attendant circumstances; yet for all purposes not purely historical or scientific, the general impression of a person or a place or an occurrence—the combined effect of all the lines, colours, forms, features, shades as we see them— goes nearest to the reality and truth. It sees with both eyes; but science and erudition scrutinize matters, as it were, artificially, with only one eye open, and with its powers often abnormally developed, thereby increasing the want of polarity and proportion and perspective in the view taken; and it is for these reasons that a good impression is always so much more valuable than the best copy or photograph. Consequently dissection and research will not be my tools. I never want to treat any part of the world as a laboratory or a library, since the examinations and explanations made in such places do not appear to me to come to sufficiently close quarters with life and humanity, which are my interests; and I am therefore usually much more inclined to put my trust boldly in feeling and imagination. Curiosity may explore and pedantry may analyze, but the soul is content to feel and absorb.

And what learning or information or reason or logic can gainsay an impression which, though the least tangible, is the strongest of human convictions? What is the lifeless, vulgar fact beside the vivid, personal impression? Is not the latter based mainly on feeling, man's first and final sense, from which all the others have been

On Traits in General

gradually evolved? For, as you know, some naturalists hold that in the dim past man felt his way even into sight, the optic nerve arising from a concentration, caused by the play of sunbeams on the seashore, of the diffused life-feeling in a blind but sensitive mass into one more especially tingling point on the surface, where it became responsive to the irritation of light; and that thus an education commenced which, carried on in it and its successors for æons, terminated in the production of an eye. Has not Coleridge, also, remarked with subtle truth how some visual impressions, such as the deep sky, are really more feelings than sights, or are at least the melting away and entire union of feeling and sight? And in somewhat the same way as the eye of the body was born, the eye of the soul, or the imagination —by the power of which we use our scattered, personal feelings and emotions in order to create out of them synthetic, impersonal thoughts and reflections—has to come into being. Man must through extreme sensitiveness *feel* his way into spiritual and intellectual sight, and so convert his own petty sensations and experiences into wide, general ideas and visions. By such sensitiveness I mean, of course, feeling coupled with perception, since the former by itself is only a matter of nerves and muscles, and but a brutish acquirement. Michael Angelo did not merely *touch* the torso that he loved to handle in his blind old age.

Accordingly, I seldom bring arguments to

convince or reasons to prove, and, indeed, I have not often seen either of these modes of exposition successful. For in a world of mystery, inexplicable in every detail, is it not waste of time and of trouble to attempt to give the actual causes, or existences, of anything? How deceptive and ignorant sight alone can be! Sugar and salt look the same. How much, too, goes on before our eyes that is wholly imperceptible. All the loveliest shades of life and light are invisible. Are even the facts that we are supposed to know reliable? Is it more than a scientific postulate to say that the earth goes round the sun? Is the human impression to the contrary less true? For are not both, earth and sun, spinning in infinite space? Has not natural religion failed to discover in the universe an absolute lord and master, whose decision between contending men would be final? Has science been able in any instance to discover really what's what? Is truth itself ever more than an impression? Is certainty more than belief? Is the mind of man capable of anything better?

Thus, in feeling and perception only can we hope to discern, to all intents and purposes, the true being of things, and their magnitude and importance must therefore always depend largely on their relation to us. The personal equation cannot be eliminated. Because a star happens to be near us we call it the sun. And in such personal impressions, based on sincere feelings and emotions, lie also what interest and originality men are capable of, either in individuality of character or in artistic expression. For originality is not necessarily newness, although as a matter of fact it is very unlikely that a genuinely sincere personality will have a duplicate. At the most the original man makes a new use of old things. His materials are usually second-hand articles, but he knows how to set them on their legs again. All through the world, then, people see much the same things—and yet with what different results! For life, both in itself as a whole, and in its endless distribution and details, affects them according to their varying dispositions, and this will be noticeable in all that they say and do. While some minds always carry within themselves their own interpretation of the world, others seem to have no powers whatever in this direction, and all the threads of life cross one another in unmeaning confusion and obscurity. Nothing, however, means, or can ever mean, the exact same to any two human beings, so marked is the impress of personality even in the weakest ; while the stronger the individuality, the less likelihood there is of there being a twin view. Owing to this—to the degree and kind of sensibility and insight and imagination which they possess — people give vastly different and vastly deeper meanings to life and all its concerns ; and the special regard which we may have for the thoughts and views of one person over those of another is to a great extent due to our own peculiar sympathies and tastes. Each writer's audience are those to whom he happens to appeal on account of some spiritual relationship or consanguinity, and, as has been truly said, the appreciative reader of a book contributes nearly as much to its power and fruitfulness as the author himself; for they are, as it were, joined in holy matrimony, and what nuptials are there more joyous and blessed? While, on the other hand, has it not been well said that 'it is not all books that are as dull as their readers?'

The facts of life, then, in so far as they are mere statistics, are there alike to all men, and only in the interpretation of their respective importance and significance rests their possible use and value. But the imaginative mind, by the power of its sensibility and perception, will always draw some meaning or purpose out of every scene or occurrence in life. For it, above all others, sees clearly and feels deeply how all the world is scroll and sign and symbol; that spirit pervades all things, giving them life and soul; that 'not a leaf is dumb;' and that 'every line we can draw on the sand has expression.' Nowhere can it find a piece of dead matter. Is it not all radiant? Has not the whole of life incalculable meanings and consequences? and at what point can its significance ever be exaggerated?

Thus, every turn that we take in life should be for its possible suggestiveness, and for no other reason. Every place we visit, every person we

On Traits in General

meet, should be so treated, since it is by so looking at every chance word and action and thought that we may come across, that a general impression or vision of the whole, based on all our sensations and experiences, begins almost unconsciously to take shape in the mind. And the area of observation need not be especially large. To an acute observer very little will tell a great deal. Often, he will in one glimpse abstract the idea, and run away with it for evermore. A person of strong feelings and emotions, though of small information and experience, sometimes perceives best the real spirit or meaning of a thing. Quiet perception sees, as a rule, far more than vulgar examination. The imaginative artist is never mathematical or, what the world calls, practical. On a sensitive organ a light touch will make a deep impression; a breath may tickle or thrill, where a blow might only crush it, or at least cause it to recoil. But carefully pick out the right little thing, and it will show you much more than itself, perhaps all. A picture, or an idea, may be the slow growth of many impressions, or they may come into being in one flash. Is it not the same in the case of people? How much more important is some small indication of character that gives a real inkling of the true nature of a person than the most elaborate acquaintance with all his words and acts. The look in a man's face often tells far more than what he says, and how much more reality have

I not seen, too, in some slight movement of his than in all his other actions put together? For usually we most of us, I fear, speak and perform for the gallery, and only now and then appears the trait which alone will influence and decide matters on crucial occasions; but it, if truly caught, is full of character and meaning. It is like an expression on the part of Nature herself made unconsciously through us. It is the fundamental, predominant fact speaking of its own accord. It is a display and an assertion of the essential, which is always a secreted power, while our ordinary words and acts, mostly ignorant and deceitful, only go to compose a worthless, confusing, and misleading compilation of stuff and nonsense.

The imaginative mind, then, luxuriates in the embryonic fertility and the symbolic wealth of the smallest things, and finds life universally suggestive. None, I believe, are more conscious of their continual indebtedness than the original and creative. The listening, seeing, feeling soul is certainly very necessary, but so also is the tell-tale object. Or it may be this way. Objects may not always give birth to directly kindred thoughts, but the countless instances of beauty and power and joy and of sorrow in the world—of nature, of art, of humanity—may, by touching a man's heart and soul, and so emotionalizing to an exceptional pitch his whole spiritual and intellectual being, inspire him generally, and thus

On Traits in General 55

rouse into activity and expression many entirely extraneous thoughts and ideas.

But, although no part of life, however small, is wholly blank and insignificant, yet we should beware of giving our attention to any one part exclusively. Though all may help, none can safely monopolize. We should not, for instance, allow ourselves to be too rigidly confined to, and tied down by, our own narrow experiences by such few stray occurrences as our lot in life chances to bring under our particular notice; but, by always giving them, through sympathetic sensibility and insight, their widest and most permanent relations, we should insist upon their helping to form and expand our general view; and not, by paying special attention to their peculiarities, permit them to lessen or contradict our previous knowledge of the universal; and unless the facts of life are to some extent seen in this light, far from their being of assistance to us in shaping and regulating our views, they are useless and positively pernicious in their crowded stagnancy.

For myself, I would be inclined to rely mainly on that knowledge which Plato says is superior to, and actually disdains mere experience, since, however great experience may be, it necessarily can cover only a comparatively small area of time and place, and can never, therefore, on the one hand, amount to much in itself, while, on the other hand, it is often just enough to impair and ruin our general knowledge or impression of the universal. But certainly the interest which we take in any situation, or scene, or event must not be for its own sake; but, by seeing its significance and wide relationship, we must convert it into a symbol or imperfect expression of much more than is apparent; and the larger and deeper the view which we take, the nearer will it go towards reaching its true and eternal relations, which are bound to be wide and extensive in a world, the philosophical solution of which is hidden somewhere in the transcendental perception of—unity underlying and binding everything, and each being an epitome of all.

To understand much rightly and blend it into one shows the truest wisdom and insight, and denotes something akin to the original strength of primeval instincts and divine intuitions. For although, as the mind of man develops, differences and subtle distinctions increase, yet as the soul grows and expands, they vanish, and in unity of conception, however unequal and unlike the range of vision and significance, the seer approaches the rustic. As 'all colours will agree in the dark,' so will all agree in the light. It is only in the dusk and the twilight that the hues and the shadows of life appear.

For the enlightened soul sees beyond, to the reconciliation of all the dark discords and contradictions which we small men live on. In its wide outlook it sees to where extremes meet and opposites

On Traits in General

unite, and harmony, or a deep sense of universal relationship owing to a mystic consciousness of identity, prevails. It cancels discrepancies and divisions, and finds sympathy and correspondence everywhere—the humanity in all men, the spirit in all things, the soul in all life, the true and the real amid the superficial and merely actual. It works, as it were, within the vast circle of life's greatest common measure. Detaching particularities, round each it discerns the halo of universal being. No land is foreign, or face strange, or situation novel, because it perceives the never-failing resemblances, even in the apparently most diverse and exceptional occurrences in the great world of humanity, where so much is ever repeating itself and returning in but slightly altered guise—echoes, memories, dreams, relations, shadows, likenesses, affinities, associations—who can escape from this inextricable maze? For there is no missing link in the perfect chain running through the whole of the world's story. Life is its own concordance; and the imaginative soul feels the symmetry of infinite space, and dwells in the harmony of the eternal *ensemble*.

So, a fact is not only a dead, dull fact, it is also a sign, a visible token of much more than is seen on the surface; and as we are not going to be content with its mere actual appearance, or body, but seek to arrive at its spirit, or representative value, it must be made to express itself in such terms. Out of the evident fact you should conjure the imaginative truth. If our experiences are not to be worthless, we must see beyond them. We should see the abstract being, or the spiritual image of a thing. As in the case of all great art, which is an image of the spirit and not an imitation of the form, we must be able to perceive more than is technically depicted, though, as a rule, since the large majority of people are absolutely literal and prosaic, the imaginative, always largely inexpressible and therefore only indicated, meets with scant notice and less understanding.

No particular instance, either, is of any use unless we can discern this spirit of which it is a partial exhibition; since this grain of abstract truth in each concrete fact alone constitutes its real value. We must winnow what we reap in the great harvest of life, if our storage is not to be mainly chaff. By this throwing aside, or submerging, of much superfluous matter, each fact, of course, will lose a good deal of its immediate bulk and importance, but what remains will be essential—and we only want the fruit and seed, or, at the most, a cutting. We do not see any use in the whole tree being laboriously uprooted and carted to—well, the fireside, since that is all that such dead lumber is fit for. The essence of a thing lies ever in the residue: it is the core, and contains its real force and life; what pith and truth it has are to be found there.

We must, then, do our best to strip the actual of its transient and particular qualities, and lay

On Traits in General 59

bare the permanent and universal. We must place events in their wide and true relations, and not merely take them as misleading circumstances and appearances may imply. Through all temporary and trivial experiences, in word, or action, or manner, we should seek the ruling traits of character and soul.

In the most varied and complicated phenomena we must endeavour to discover the pervading idea, the central mainspring. In all persons and places we should look beyond the superficial and irrelevant, which are so very obtrusive, to the hidden, deep, and essential. Among the endless facts and figures of life, we ought to distinguish those that are of real consequence from those that are of only momentary importance. However great your information and learning may be, your imagination should carry you further, into a world of promise and possibility; and, so, your work, though based on and using much knowledge of the past and experience of the present, will run a chance of being lasting and true of the future. In order to generalize with interest and value about anything, one must see it as it is, and as it was, and as it will be.

But you should not go too far from the actual, and perhaps lose your way. However deep you go, or high you mount, you should always be able to trace your way back to it if necessary. Nor, for my part, should I care to indulge in direct prophecies any more than I should be inclined to believe in those of others. Time is the only prophet that I know of, and only the predictions of posterity would be worth listening to. The greatest contemporary is much too handicapped for me to put any trust in him.

Yet would I fain see behind things,—spirit and substance are so much more than form and details. Is not the spirit that built, and that has since contemplated and adored the splendid shrines and cathedrals of the Middle Ages greater than the buildings themselves? However beautiful, are they more than the inferior embodiment of the divine aspirations of the soul? For spiritual vision alone sees the true beauty of the world. The clever eye and the bright intelligence, culture and learning, however remarkable, do not see more than the empty effigy—the shell of the egg. And barren and impotent are all the scenes and experiences of life if they do not breed ideas, the true generation of the world; and worse than useless are they if they are allowed to accumulate like so much undigested matter, causing a spiritual constipation in the soul. What is the greatest body and bulk of information, if feeling and character and imagination are lacking? Suppose the range of knowledge wide, but what if there is no fire in the range? These things avail not, in my opinion. I do not care for the stuffed head of man or beast, bison or botanist. Deformed and unsightly in my eyes are all such *disjecta membra;* a little real life, personal force and

On Traits in General 61

substance, are more than the best trophies that learning or sport can produce.

Thus, in themselves, all the facts of life repel and repress me, though the spirit and influences that they generate swell and sway me. For what, in truth, is the good of merely knowing things, especially when so many of these things are so insignificant and irrelevant? Why this pedantic exactitude, and all these minute and uninteresting details? Are they not an oppressive and noxious superfluity at all times, and to-day more than ever? Wholesale, indiscriminating love of information is, to my mind, one of the very worst diseases of modern life, injurious both to society and to the individual.

Most people seem to take some mad, insatiable pleasure in getting to know quickly, by various means—letters, telegrams, newspapers—endless items of a manifestly trivial and transitory description, and therefore at no time, early or late, worth knowing. Is it any wonder that the philosopher is driven to saying: 'Once for all, there is much I do *not* want to know. Wisdom sets bounds even to knowledge'? And, although he may doubtless often have to plead guilty, with apparent shame, to ignorance of many of these facts and details, I will add this, by way of justification, that on such occasions he generally finds, I think, that he knows something much greater—for he knows how uninteresting and unimportant it is to know these things. Cumbersome and utterly useless, in his eyes, are at least half of those numerous facts of time and history and experience, and arbitrary enumerations of place and person and event, with which we cram our heads, and which, since they do not appeal in any way to our moral and intellectual judgment, have just to be mechanically learnt and remembered. And how very inferior is all such learning and information, depending, as they do, almost entirely on industry, and memory, and erudition, to that intuitive wisdom which is born of character and soul! 'That is the face of a very amiable gentleman, but I don't know who it is,' said Emerson, as, when his memory was failing him, but not his insight into character, he looked at the body of his dead friend, Longfellow.

In itself, the dullest thing in the world is a statistical fact, or a mere name, or occurrence, or date. All the performances and arrangements in life, however complex and novel, have never, for their own sakes, roused any special interest or astonishment in me. You may have wondered how ships were built, or how prisons were conducted, or how oysters were procured and packed; but I have seen all these things, and many more less common, and I have never yet come across anything exceptionally extraordinary or unintelligible. And these qualities, indeed, in all matters, you either find in abundance at your own hall-door, or, if not, then you will never find them, though you should travel the whole

On Traits in General

world over. All the affairs of ordinary, practical life, however distant and foreign, just manage, like anything else, to take place somehow. That is all about it. There is nothing more to know or to see. And he must be, therefore, a very ignorant and illiterate neophyte who would dream of finding a scrap of real novelty or peculiarity in any of the scenes and situations of such life, since in no sphere of it is there more than the result of a little common-sense and experience. The mechanism of living and doing—its many shifts and plans and dodges—is fairly simple and evident, even in a scientific age.

No; you must look deeper, if you seek strange and interesting and peculiar things—into the very heart and soul of conscious man, into the mystic regions of personality, profoundly significant, solemn, and wonderful, bordering on divinity. Here alone, too, is there a possibility of lighting on the rich mine of individuality, so precious and rare in life and in art. For ordinarily the words and acts and thoughts of men are very much the same. Although you may not have thought so, and may even proceed to recount what you consider to be a peculiar chapter of accidents and experiences, nevertheless I venture to say that in the wide sphere outside personal consciousness—and that is not a marked feature in many—all men have done whatever has been done by any man, if not actually, then sufficiently in conception and spirit, and are therefore to this large extent—and it may be the whole ground—similar, if not identical. For we have not yet by any means reached that more advanced and perfect stage in the history, or evolution, of the race, when there will be as many distinct specimens of humanity as there are human beings in the world, when originality, or genuineness, will appear in all that we say and do. We shall, I fear, have to wait a little longer before men are more different than sheep from one another.

IV.

I, therefore, for good or for bad, willingly gave myself up in my travels to my own unsophisticated impressions, and am accordingly aware—and it is a matter of some misgiving with me—that the value of my remarks, in the eyes of others, must depend almost entirely on what reliance they are ready to put on my powers of observation and discernment.

These, then, are the itinerant impressions and reflections at random of a passing traveller—only two short months in the States. Of the many vagrant thoughts that crowded on me, as we hurriedly went from place to place, these are the few that now, as I look back, stand out in bold and prominent relief. Recurring often to my mind, they have become settled and dogmatic convictions. They are reflections, or the culmination of much sensibility and emotion in the past. For our thoughts and feelings are to the mental and spiritual frame what food and drink are to the

On Traits in General 65

body, and reflections are what is retained and assimilated, and thereby becomes a constituent and conscious part of our intellectual being. They are the quintessence of a man's history and experience.

These are, too, the nearest approach to facts that I can produce, since, taking only a cursory and unconfirmed glance, one cannot exactly vouch for everything, although all that I say is based on what I saw and felt, and I should be sorry to think that it had not a good foundation in reality. A longer visit might perhaps have changed or modified some of my opinions, but naturally I am inclined to think that it would only have confirmed and strengthened them.

I, of course, leave unmentioned many kindnesses received and many little personal matters, more fit for conversation than print; and I hope that on the whole I give no cause for offence in what I say, as it is the last thing I should like to do to so obliging and hospitable a people. In this connection it is, indeed, far from my intention to bless or to curse anyone, nor do I wish to draw any invidious comparisons between different countries. Again, many things that one notices, as though they were peculiar to the land one is travelling in, possibly apply more or less to other nations and places as well, since I am sure that one is greatly inclined in foreign parts to note as strange what is often a common enough sight at home. As a visitor, one is struck with and one's attention is called to what, as a resident, one has never observed or heard referred to.

Certainly this is especially likely to be the case in any contrast between the inhabitants of these islands and the Americans; for were there ever two people so like and yet so unlike, having so much in common—the same blood and religion and language—and yet so different? For what freedom and variety have not the Yankees introduced into these very similarities, thus almost completely transforming them! It is true that they speak the same language, but what of all the new words and idioms, tones and inflexions? Is the nasal twang nothing? Is their slang not a new language in itself? They may, too, have the same religion or religions, but how much more numerous and pronounced are their variations and extravagances in this respect! And, even if they are of the same blood, and have at bottom many of the same instincts and tastes, still they have many strongly-marked idiosyncrasies of their own. New shoots have been grafted on the old stem. Characteristic differences in their physical appearance, even in the complexion of the skin, in the training and education and the manners and relations of the two sexes, and in the aims and customs of their whole social and political life, have started and developed.

In spite, therefore, of the near kinship and fundamental similarity, it would not, I think, be advisable to draw too close a comparison between

On Traits in General 67

these two great English-speaking nations; for, as someone has truly said, 'Between things most like unto each other, semblance telleth the most beautiful lies.' It would not, I believe, teach us any useful lessons, for, owing to their respective positions in the history of the world, there is really no true analogy between them. Doubtless we are influencing one another for our mutual good, but let no one suppose that, because we do speak the same tongue, and are of the same stock, and have got the same faith, that therefore what is found suitable in the one place can be applied to the other with a like result. For these two countries are as different from each other as 'a woman with a past' is from a young lady of fifteen.

We have a past, and, whether we like it or not, it is part of our present. We cannot escape from it. However dead or antiquated many of our old habits and traditions may seem, they must be accepted and counted on in all calculations by even the most extreme Radical. If he is wise, he will recognise that his home is haunted, and that he himself is of ancient lineage. But the Americans are a regenerated race, and they have no ghosts.

AMERICAN TRAITS.

' Friends of America, look over the Atlantic Sea,
A bended bow is lifted in heaven, and a heavy iron chain
Descends link by link from Albion's cliffs across the sea
    to bind
Brothers and sons of America, till our faces pale and yellow,
Heads deprest, voices weak, eyes downcast, hands work-
    bruised,
Feet bleeding on the sultry sands, and the furrows of the
    whip,
Descend to generations that in future times forget.'
                                                         BLAKE.

' Have the elder races halted?
Do they droop and end their lesson, wearied over there
    beyond the seas?
We take up the task eternal, and the burden, and the
    lesson,
        Pioneers! O pioneers!

' All the past we leave behind,
We debouch upon a newer, mightier world, varied world.
Fresh and strong the world we seize, world of labour and
    the march,
        Pioneers! O pioneers!'
                                                    WHITMAN.

AMERICAN TRAITS.

I.

THE United States have advanced greatly, by leaps and bounds 'commensurate with Niagara,' since the days when they were known as our American Colonies, and the inhabitants of those distant settlements were supposed to hold their land as in the manor of East Greenwich, near London, and to be represented in Parliament by the members of the county and borough which contained that manor. Nevertheless, they are still a young people in a new country, and their history has not only to be written, but even to be made. The *Mayflower*—saved from the deluge that spread over England in the seventeenth century—is the Noah's Ark of the New World, while, as a nation, the States have existed for little more than a hundred years. They are, indeed, scarcely out of the womb of national conception, and mother and child do not as yet seem to know one another properly.

So everything is fresh and young and early and promising. The world is still, so to speak, 'in the beginning.' There are no oaks, but there are plenty of acorns. They have excellent breakfasts, but they have no afternoon tea; they have not reached that time of day at all. There is no past worth speaking about, but there is a future well worth thinking about. In no way can the country be said to be mature or classical, nor has it any of the equipment or associations of age or custom or tradition. It is not a growth, and there are as yet hardly any legitimate results or consequences. It was discovered one fine morning, and soon after abruptly started on a civilized basis; and neither event took place very long ago. Parts of the West are contemporaneous with last night's mushrooms. Rome was not built in a day, but Chicago was. Time has not so far been able to produce a genuine ruin; you must give it time. I saw no moss; and the ivy had not reached the top of the wall. The country still suffers visibly from its almost premature birth, and will need much care and coaxing to recover and arrive at its full stature and development. In fine, to say briefly what, though probably heard before, personal experience and observation strongly confirmed:—the United States is no ancient historical playground or mediæval demesne of romance; it is not the home of princes and nobles, of churches and shrines, of castles and galleries. It is no fairyland, rich in legends and

American Traits

myths. Antiquities and curiosities, miniatures and heirlooms, do not abound, and are not indigenous; your grandfather's bust looks nearly as old there as the Elgin Marbles do here. The only relics in the country are living specimens of the wild life of former days—the Indian and the buffalo—and they are becoming very scarce; a few may still be seen in the Reserves and the National Park—great open-air museums where these handsome mementos of a bygone age are kept and protected at the public expense. In this broad, flat, open country there are no interesting holes or corners, or nooks or crannies; there is little that is picturesque or artistic, or out of the way or off the common. Finally, there are no persons, nor are there any 'splendid paupers.'

No, this is the land of the people, and of some inglorious millionaires; of cities and citizens, of stores and offices, factories and institutions, trains and trams, bells and wires; of clerks and artizans, lawyers and politicians, manufacturers and miners, speculators and merchants, butchers and brokers —in short, of countless faces, facts, and figures. Industry and trade, labour and capital, stocks, shares, trusts, rings, pools, strikes, monopolies and syndicates, money and business—these are the powers that reign and rule. And I remember well how in New York City, instead of spending one's time as a stranger would in London—in visiting such places as the British Museum, or the National Gallery, or Westminster Abbey, or the Tower—we passed a long day on Blackwell Island, going over gaols, reformatories, hospitals and asylums, and seeing, in every shape and form, idiots, lunatics, criminals, and invalids; and, in my opinion, the way in which we spent that day in the metropolis of the States was most characteristic of the country and of its peculiar interests; and it helps, I think, to show how very different, and even opposed, are the specialities and excellences of the Old and the New Worlds. The typical sights and objects in America are eminently social and economic.

Of some such sort, then, is the kingdom of 'the West and Modern,' and, even as such, I was anxious to visit it. For, right or wrong, the Americans are the destined pioneers of our civilization. They are the chosen people of the coming century, and their country has long been the land of promise. A writer is not much anticipating the importance of the Republic when, speaking of some event that influenced it, he adds, 'and therefore the world.' Accordingly, I looked forward with great interest and curiosity, and with many hopes, to seeing the social and political life and the traits of character of these seventy millions of independent, self-governing human beings; and I am quite certain that no one who has not a genuine love for humanity—not merely as it manifests itself here and there in particular individuals, but generally as an idea and a whole—will derive much pleasure or profit from a visit to the United States. If you have not a deep and sincere faith in mankind as a race, and a broad, democratic sympathy with all human efforts and struggles, keep away from this vast mob of undistinguished and indistinguishable people. It is but a colourless crowd of barren existence to the dilettante, a poisonous field of clover to the cynic.

II.

And, first, as to the general appearance of the country itself. How wild and unsettled it is—the irregular houses, the scattered fields, the unkept roads, the tangled woods—all without finish or fence! Even in New England, forests and underwood cover every inch of soil that is not in cultivation; and the forests there are natural woods, not planted trees. A wide, rough tract of waste and wood; of distant hills and hidden glades, which only wild Indians and deer could adorn properly; with here and there a village or farmhouse, all constructed out of the surrounding timber. The country is still so sparsely occupied that, once you leave the large towns, each habitation or village looks like a new settlement, an oasis in the midst of an uninhabited and unexplored region.

There are no neighbours; no one ever heard of such a thing as 'a neighbourhood!' There are no real homes, with home interests and cares. The people are 'located;' they know of no closer tie to a place. Even the best residences are only great log-huts luxuriously furnished. None of the buildings are substantial and lasting. The architecture everywhere is rickety and temporary. There are no coping-stones. The occupants evidently have no intention of permanently settling down there. Indeed, you will meet with nothing straight or orderly in this great, crooked country, unless it be the streets in the large cities. Society is higgledy-piggledy; the bulk of the population are nondescript; everything is at sixes and sevens. Definition and distinction are a long way off yet: even to the oldest natives, America is still a *terra incognita*. The colloquialisms are significant. No wonder the people ' guess ' most things: the whole country is one immense framework of guesses.

It is so large and varied and profuse. Here the East and the West collide, and the North vies with the South. It is the child of all nations and the mother of every description of stranger and exile. Every language finds its spokesman there. Peopled from all parts of the globe, civilized and uncivilized, it contains and has absorbed every mixture and variety of the human race, from the pale and bilious New Yorker, ' of a horrible whiteness,' to the stout and swarthy Southerner; from the curly, undressed crop of the nigger, to such a tonsorial opposite as the sleek, pomatumed hair of the Yankee. The people are a race of cosmopolitan quadroons. In this land of universal *entrée* and welcome—till of late years—the anti-

American Traits

podes of humanity, in blacks and whites or in the Irish and the Chinese, live side by side and under the same roof, like the prairie-dog and owl in the one burrow.

It sports every climate under the sun, from arctic cold to torrid heat; a swallow need not leave its shores the whole year round; sweeping cyclones follow parching droughts; prairie fires and blizzards alternate; heated air and iced water go together. Every lavish, copious phrase, such as, 'There are more fish in the sea than ever came out of it,' applies to it and helps to describe, or at least suggest, the marvellous fecundity, the countless riches and resources of this huge, undeveloped, prolific, abounding country. There is nothing small or niggardly in it, nor is there anything mean or scanty about this flush, well-fed people. There is no Poor Law—they are too much alive to require any living mortuaries. Wages are high by custom and by law; it is a criminal offence to import a coolie or a labourer hired under contract elsewhere. A bounteous prodigality and generosity shows itself on all sides. There are thirteen to every dozen. The margin is never reached, but, on the contrary, how to dispose of immense fortunes and surpluses is a question of considerable difficulty both to individuals and to the nation at large. Far from having to devise means of raising money in order to pay off a national debt, one of the differences between the two great political parties is about how it were best to spend a surplus and keep down the revenue in future; while the splendid munificence of some of the millionaires, in starting and endowing such noble institutions as, say, the Drexel Institute and Girard College, is well-known and acknowledged with universal admiration. For, although a Yankee would be the last man in the world to look upon the city of his birth or residence as his country or nation, or only home, and to consider all other places exile, as Dante did Bologna and Verona, nevertheless he takes a great and worthy pride in it, and often shows in this laudable way a truly practical and patriotic interest in it. Of course they are, one and all, a city-loving people. Everyone hails from some town or other. Did you ever meet an American who came from a country part? And I remember how strange it seemed to them when we did not mention some town as our home. And as for their spurious efforts at country life—they are the most pitiable cases of *urbs in rure*. And, of course, you know how all Americans over here are cockneys—if not *ipsis cockniensibus cockniores*.

Everything, too, is on so huge and grand a scale—from Niagara downwards. The woods are forests; the farms, ranches; the lakes, seas. Tornadoes or conflagrations demolish entire cities, and that more than once. Indeed, an American town is hardly entitled to call itself one until it has been wrecked or burnt to the ground at least three times. Even a village is, as they say, 'the biggest little city of its size.' And who has not been impressed by the appearance of New York City—that monstrous growth on the island of Manahatta—when, after passing through the Narrows, one first sees its colossal buildings, or 'sky-scrapers,' as they are called? Many of these have more than twenty stories, one above the other, and tower high over the loftiest steeples and spires. It looked to me like a city on stilts. I had often heard of castles in the air, but I had never before dreamt of, much less seen, plain common houses and offices in the air.

And this great country, stretching from the Atlantic shore to the Pacific slope, and in many ways standing for the whole continent of America, delineates with proportionate spaciousness the rest of the world, recognising but two seas, its lateral oceans, and but two other countries, Europe and Asia. Proud of my own little country, and exclusive in my racial and national affections, I had not imagined that I could ever be looked upon as only a European; but in the United States one soon perceives that one has stepped out of insularity into continentality, from nationalism to federalism. For there, not an island, not even a State, puts bounds to patriotism, or to local feelings and associations. The President and Congress, in the exercise of their respective powers, control many distant States, from Washington to Florida, and from Maine to California. People of widely differing origin and habits and beliefs live under similar laws and customs, like some gigantic 'happy family' of the human race. In Congress, the provincial prejudices and peculiarities of forty-five separate States meet and have to coalesce somehow.

In this vast federation, with its one supreme executive officer and legislature, such variations as exist among the many branches of the human race —nearly all of which are represented there—are ignored, and the great underlying, elemental, spinal similarities that are shared alike by all civilized human beings are acknowledged and acted on. That is a remarkable trait of American government. In their broad and liberal administration they are anxious to discover and satisfy the many universal qualities which we all have, however superficially different we may be, rather than to accentuate the few variations and idiosyncrasies which separate individuals and races.

When the Republic was started, it was founded on a theoretical axiom which, if not actually true, has at any rate won favour and support for the great truth that there are many elements and factors common to all humanity. So, the people of each State cordially recognise that they are all citizens of one country. State freedom and independence have not been found incompatible with national unity and integrity. Be the political parties Democratic or Republican, or anything else, they are all National. For the Americans see that, though the number of stars on their national flag—one for each State—may increase, there can never be more than one sun, the unbroken standard of the Union.

III.

You do not cross the Atlantic ocean to find pearls of saline spray, nor do you visit the American republic to meet persons of striking individuality. You have come to the land of 'government of the people, by the people, and for the people.' The citizen is the undisputed sovereign, and he has no subjects or superiors, but each has an equal voice in the affairs of the country. There are no menials, either by profession or in manner. No one serves; some help. There are poor people; there are unfortunate people; but there are no beggars. Every man stands for himself, and for no more or less; none are crowned, but each man carries his sovereignty under the crown of his own hat. All *primi inter pares*—it is like some great confraternity. It is an insult to tip a typical American; a man will give you a lift on with your coat or answer a civil question gratuitously. All are in the same box. It is the realm of the average man; there is no other sort. 'One man is as good as another,' says the Yankee, and he sees no reason to add the subtle corollary of the Irishman—'and betther!' The people seemed to me like a great mob of common jurors, for there is certainly nothing special about any of them. It is the land of the oi πολλοί with a vengeance. There are oysters in abundance, but they have little flavour. Nothing rises above the common level but some gigantic buildings and 'the Elevated' in New York.

In this huge panorama of humanity the individual is never more than a mite among midgets. There are no titles or privileges of station or rank, but each man is entitled to his own person and property and name, in full, and without any priority or interference. Bishops and mayors even are not lords. There are no nobles, but every one is ennobled by the patent of human birthright. They have never heard of any distinction between a gentleman and any other man. There are no snobs, and there is no precedence; whoever is nearest to the door goes out first, without any gesticulations or dubiety. You take your place in the queue.

Yet there are some Americans who are very proud of their ancestry, and who are never tired of boasting that a progenitor of theirs went over in the *Mayflower*. So many, indeed, do so, that it is a notorious matter of astonishment in naval circles what a large and prolific cradle of the race that celebrated vessel must have been. In fact, it is quite evident that we have greatly deteriorated in ship-building since those days; while Shoolbred's and Maple's would not hold all the old tables and chairs and chests that are gravely pointed out as having been part of the ship's furniture.

In talking of 'the people,' then, it must not be supposed that I refer to any particular class or section, such as we have—nobility, or gentry, or middle-classes, or peasantry—since in the States 'the people,' though undoubtedly a wholesale, is nevertheless a perfectly clear and definite designation, embracing the entire population of the country, with just the insignificant exception of a small so-called fashionable set, who, by deliberately buying themselves out, have ceased to be representative of their country, and have become little artificial coteries by themselves, and who are thoroughly uninteresting and unimportant. 'A sort of high-life-below-stairs business' an American writer has truly called it. For America is a great and an interesting country, of all countries in the world perhaps the greatest in its people, but the least interesting in its upper classes. 'Our American superiority and vitality,' says the same writer, 'are in the bulk of the people, not in the gentry, like the old world. The greatness of our army during the Secession war was in the rank and file, and so with the nation.' In fact, speaking more generally, they have no classes—upper or lower; and this is a remarkable trait, and its effects can be seen throughout the whole of the life and society and the manners and opinions of the people. Especially does this strike one who has been educated in Europe, where the feeling of class-distinction is so strong a factor in all social and political life, being an hereditary and an almost essential part of our traditional and actual, and of our religious, teaching. But respect or reverence for any sort of personal superiority or eminence, even when it is intellectual and moral, and therefore worthy of it, does not exist in the States.

It is, then, the land of the people *en masse*, and the people are the public. All are included, and no one person more than another. Even on the trains there are no classes. There is everywhere a free-and-easy comradeship—even between the two sexes; witness, for example, the charming, platonic friendship of the summer-girl of Narragansett, who acts as a companion to a young man during his holiday. There is a general familiarity, as if all the people were near neighbours, although in reality that is probably very far from being the case. Everything is as public and as loud as their long, noisy railroad cars. All sorts and conditions of men live on the same footing, and on the same flat, and few have hall-doors of their own. In this great amphitheatre there are no enclosures; there are no preserves. Every park is a common; every path a thoroughfare. The country houses are surrounded by verandas, and every window is a door. There are no walls or hedges—only an occasional paling. So, no one can ever exceed the limits of private grounds or property. There is no forbidden fruit—certainly apples are not. No one can poach; no one can trespass—not that there is any desire to do so, although you might have supposed that, since there was so much room for all, a man would be anxious to enclose a piece of ground for himself exclusively. But that is not the case. Human nature acts contrariwise, and is liberal and generous only where there is plenty for all; but, when the pinch comes, it is then that it is covetous, and jealously protects its own by warnings and prosecutions. But this is the country of the open road, where no one ever met with a barrier or demesne-wall, or a *cul de sac*. The inhabitants of that illimitable land have not yet nearly reached the end of their long tether. They are still, in all matters, far from the *ultima Thule* of their vast new world. Behind every ultimate there is another. In that great free land—free especially in the way of size and room—there is breathing-space for all, and many more. Everybody can squat in comfort and ease there. The country is not yet entirely allotted, much less hopelessly subdivided; being, in this respect, very unlike home, where we are so crowded together, always in the way of one another, often treading on our neighbour's feet, and occasionally even pressing hard on his sore points. I can well say so, living, as I do, a part of the year in London, and the rest of it in the middle of a congested district in Ireland.

There is, however, a scandalous exception to this general equitable treatment in the case of the coloured population, or blacks—the *bête noire* of the country—who are cruelly excluded, not by law, but by universal custom, from participation in most of the political and social rights enjoyed by their neighbours. If they are no longer, since the Civil War, helots, they are, nevertheless, still looked upon as βάρβαροι. A white will not serve a black in his home, or in a hotel or restaurant, no matter how well paid; and even charitable institutions put 'white' among the qualifications necessary for admission. The feelings and reminiscences of unquestioned domination in the past are still strong. Is not the shameful practice of lynch law a remnant of the slavery days? Under the cloak of expiating some hideous crime, the whites seek to assert and keep alive their old tyranny over the blacks, who are thus savagely punished by their quondam masters, as though they were abnormal monsters alone guilty in these ways—as though their worst offences were not a common item in the criminal calendars of civilized nations. But, in this manner, the South seeks to maintain and exercise some of the power it once legally possessed; and, in my opinion, the great and noble cause of abolition will not be really triumphant until all these feelings and customs have entirely died out or been suppressed, and the blackest negro gets fair play. 'I am black, but, oh, my soul is white,' he cries, and the Americans will have yet to listen.

IV.

And in this land of many currents life is a weathercock, that may at any moment turn in a new direction, and the people know it, and are always on the watch. In so large an area of choice and venture, there is no reason why, if you go to the wall, you should not find an aperture somewhere and begin life all over again on a fresh and different plane. There is sure to be plenty of elbow-room anyhow, and so you can always strike out, if you like, on a new line. Ever happy-go-lucky—for much does go lucky in that fortunate country—the ambitious youth does not make a dead set at a fixed object. There are too many balls rolling for any particular one to receive his sole and undivided attention. He only determines to get on somehow.

Although a keen business people, the Americans are not especially persevering in their work, except when success is within their grasp, when they are very tenacious; but, in reaching it, they will shift about in the most haphazard manner from one occupation to another, and with astonishing courage and smoothness. They will rotate this way and that, and with remarkable ease,—just as they do when dancing. For they know how to reverse; and in one dance, also, they will change partners many times; and these fashions are characteristic of more important concerns. Compared to a John Bull, a Yankee is a Jackanapes of a man. No doubt the English are a successful and practical people, but only if left plodding along in the old beaten tracks; and their deficiencies in brightness and quickness are very evident when they are compared with the alert, ready, resourceful practicality of the Americans. Perhaps the day of the bull-dog is drawing to a close, and the greyhound is now about to have his day. Perhaps no longer is 'the battle to the strong,' but 'the race is to the swift.'

Certainly slow and steady progress is not the Yankee's mode of getting on, for he is no pattern of patience and perseverance. He makes his horses trot fast, and he does not in the least admire the snail's pace. He never uses steps or stairs, but at one bound either is elevated to the top or sinks to the bottom. If he does not succeed immediately at one trade or profession, he quickly moves on to some other, and so on. Any route will do. He does not think more of one than of another. Accordingly, you will find the same man a saddler one day and a senator another; one day a schoolmaster, and the next a harbourmaster; a professor of mathematics at one time, and of law at another; now an attorney, and now an ambassador; now a surveyor, and now a journalist; to-day the keeper of a dry-goods store, and tomorrow the Governor of a State; now a boatman on a river, and now the President of the country.

The professions, also, are not so specialized as they are with us. Every lawyer is both a solicitor and a barrister. The Civil Service offices are always changing hands. Politics are professional, and professions are political. The true Yankee, in fact, is a Jack-of-all-trades; he has generally had a go at each one of them in turn.

He has also the whole of life to work in, for he begins early and never for one moment stops; he seldom takes any vacation, long or short. The Yankees are a nation of clerks. They know of no entrance into life but the tradesman's, and firmly believe that there is no admission into Heaven except on business. There is never any necessity to tell an American boy to stick close to his desk. He has no desire or temptation to play truant. Like a duck to the water, he straightway plunges into business. After leaving college he willingly takes up his position on a stool for life, being in that respect very unlike his contemporaries here, who require years of cruel weaning before they recover from the loss of their beloved *alma mater*. And business will occupy him exclusively and up to the very end of his life. He will die sitting at his desk, with a cheque in his hands and a pen behind his ear. His last words will be *litera scripta*, probably an endorsement, and he will die young into the bargain; for the wages of such work is early death.

Plato complained that those who pursue philosophy at all, do so only in the intervals of housekeeping and business. But a Yankee has no such intervals even. He is nothing but a clerk, a partner in some firm, and he has neither time nor inclination to attend to the affairs of his intellect and soul. Many of them, indeed, do not seem to be aware of there being anything else in the world but money-making, so that with justice and truth has it been said that what American humanity is most in danger of is 'an overwhelming prosperity —business, worldliness, materialism.' Certainly the Americans, as a people, cannot be said to be addicted to philosophical or intellectual pursuits. Looking at matters from quite a low point of view, I think they are on this score peculiarly deficient.

The men, as I have said, are too much engaged in business to find time or opportunities to read, or reflect on, anything outside the four walls of their offices. To be sure, the ladies boast greatly of their accomplishments in this direction, and there is no doubt that they possess whatever literary and artistic culture and taste there is in the country, just as they also do all the travelling, and can reap the educational advantages that there are to be gained in that way; for, ordinarily, the wife and daughters have been to London and Paris and Stratford-on-Avon and Bayreuth, while the husbands and sons have never left their desks. But this comparative excellence on the part of the women does not amount to much in my opinion, and I am certain that a false impression of its magnitude and importance is given, owing to the entire absence of intellectual training and attainments in the male portion of the community.

A lady who has read enough of Ruskin or of Herbert Spencer to enable her to prate about them ignorantly seems a prodigy of learning to a man who has never heard of them. But only beside him and in his eyes does this 'little knowledge' appear so abnormal and wonderful, and to me it will always seem a great pity—even a disaster, injurious to both sexes—that the American men should allow themselves to remain inferior to the women in these important matters. For, as it is, the women, since they do all the reading and travelling, easily lead in and monopolise the entire intellectual and social life of the country, and the men are nowhere. A petticoat is far the most powerful passport to American society; as for trousers, they are the livery of lacqueys, a badge of natal shame and degradation. At least, so I judged both from the servile behaviour of the men themselves and from the manner in which they are treated by the ladies. But petticoats entitle the bearer, or wearer, to the first place in every discussion, and the conversation at a party is often nothing but a lecture from an American girl. She is a perpetual *prima donna*. No one else can talk, for she never stops. As Mr. Henry James says, 'one feels her presence too much as a sound,' and that is dull and disappointing, and is not the truest or the wisest mode of feminine assertion. At home only cocks crow, and a female attempting to do so is not natural or attractive. Argumentative and positive, and at the same time ignorant and illogical, it is neither sweet unreasonableness nor clever blue-stockingism. But so much for the typical American girl on her native pavement.

v.

Thus wear and tear is the American motto. Time and toil are synonymous and ceaseless. A man will give you an appointment at midnight. Leisure is undreamt of in their philosophy of life. They never retire. Ex-judges and ex-presidents go back to the Bar. They have no homes to retire to—no other interests to occupy them. For they live largely in hotels which, *à l'Americaine,* supply them with every domestic necessity and comfort. To a Yankee the hotel of his choice is for the time being his domicile. He does not think that there is no place like home, either as a matter of sentiment or in reality—for very often he has none. He is a rolling stone, and he gathers no moss with which to build himself a nest. Many of them live in trains, which are always well stocked with the provisions, if not luxuries, of living. Everything is in motion; there are few fixtures. Entire houses even are moved on rollers from one site to another. The country is no haven of peace and quiet; the people dislike what is stationary. An American said that he did not mind dying, but it was being dead so long that was so terrible. Their heavenly desire is not to 'rest in peace.' They dread eternity if that is what it means; for they are not yet worn out or tired; there are no *décadents;*

and they wish for no rest—unless it be the sleep of a spinning-top. So, a man is here to-day, and he is off to-morrow—perhaps to the other end of the world, or perhaps only a thousand miles, to an adjacent town; and it is nearly the same with his house and goods. He 'expresses' his luggage or furniture, and hurries ahead himself unencumbered; or, perchance, he may have his business in one city, and his home in another, hundreds of miles away, as when a man wishes to keep the fashionable life of his wife and daughters a thing apart from the tradesman's life of himself and his sons. Thus the whole population, like a race of civilized gipsies, is ever on the move. In this wild, uncultivated country grass grows nowhere—certainly not under their feet. For they would outstrip their own shadows. Swift of foot, like Hiawatha hastening forward after shooting, their arrows almost fall behind them. From hanging upwards, they would do everything by electricity. They never walk when they can drive, and they will never drive when they can fly. In the cities they never stop to talk, and they could not hear one another if they did; and in the country you will seldom see, even a man alone, with less than two horses and four wheels conveying him. They are, I fear, in no way peripatetic philosophers. He who runs may read—but they never do either. Hurry and reflection, or thought and noise, do not thrive together.

Thus, they have recourse to every conceivable

form of speed and locomotion, although the tremendous use that they make of the telephone saves them a great deal of the latter. In the towns there are, besides the ordinary vehicles, innumerable horse-trams and electric cars—cable and trolly—and New York City has, in addition, the 'Elevated,' and is about to make an 'Underground.' The people strive to move faster than time, just as by their splendid train-service they have already, one may say, conquered space. Indeed, these two infinities have almost been reduced by them to finite grasp and comprehension. And these railroads, spreading over the whole country, are the advancing lines of civilization, along which new towns rapidly grow up, owing to which circumstance—that the towns are built after the railroads have been made, and not, as it is with us, the railways made between existing towns—has arisen the very awkward and dangerous difficulty of level crossings. Some cities are simply overrun with trains; even in the middle of crowded streets they are often on the same level as the houses, and the poor pedestrian walks in constant risk of being run over by some train, or electric tram. You are, in fact, safe nowhere—unless in one of them. For apparently these democratic means of locomotion may kill with perfect impunity. Lives and limbs are of small concern where there is nothing more important than despatch—the victim of which is often a human life. So, without any compunction

American Traits

or compensation, they will ride clean over every obstacle, beast or man. The brake is never put on, except when the destination is reached; they can admit of no interruption, and will only stop to suit themselves. Some of the electric cars have trays, like the cow-catchers on engines in the West, attached in front, which may possibly let you off with severe injuries only, and that is the most that you can hope for—and the ox on the prairie gets as much.

The truth is that, in a country where there is so much to do and to get, no one can afford to turn aside even for a second, and so reckless, unchecked progression has become the undeviating order of march throughout its length and breadth. Delay is defeat. There is no time to stop, because there is none to lose. And, in my opinion, the mercurial qualities of the American born and raised—the briskness and indefatigable activity—are not, as is often supposed, due to the nature of the climate, but are rather to be attributed to the fact that he is, and has been for some time, living in a new, undeveloped, and, in parts, undiscovered country. The early bird gets the worm—and there are here many worms to be got. First come, first served—and there is here always something to be served. It is this —the fact that there are so many prizes to win, and fortunes to be found—that keeps up his unflagging energy and spirits; for, as long as there is any breath in him, a Yankee will not give up. It is objects that stimulate business and life; it is plums that make a pie. As for the climate, I did not find it especially invigorating.

But in this rich, promising land the spirit of venture is everywhere. There is no limit to ambition, no more than there is to the territory. The men are content with no fortune and with no home. Restless rovers, ever seeking reduplication, they do not appreciate the prudential maxim that says the half is more than the whole. In America a bird in the hand is not worth two in the bush. Such proverbs—the wisdom of an ancient, if not exhausted, civilization—are not applicable in a new country. So, the people are not satisfied with keeping what they have, as we are only too thankful to be able to do; and they would not even have the patience to wait for the compound interest which the Irishman desired, when he said that he would have half first and the whole afterwards. They would have and risk all at once. And in this respect the vicissitudes of a typical American career are very strange to our eyes. Fortunes are made and lost over and over again by the same man. The alternate ups and downs of life are striking and terrible. 'Heads or tails!'—a toss-up is almost a daily occurrence. There is no putting by for a rainy day; for they see no clouds or threatening signs in their azure sky. All things are ever in the act of being turned over for the thousandth time. For, not merely to make a living comfortably or even luxuriously,

American Traits

but to amass a fortune and double and redouble it is the duty of every male member of the community. The one desire is to gain. With them to acquire and increase are not means but ends in themselves; not that they are by nature sordid or miserly, but because in this money-making world to collect and pile up has become a second nature to them. Their pleasure lies in the keen rivalry of speculation and enterprise, and not in the peaceful rest and enjoyment of affluence. Jay Gould was, after all, only a remarkable example of a very common type of man, since the time and ability of nearly every Yankee are absorbed in gambling transactions. Speculation is the very breath of their life and being, and it soon degenerates into mere trickery and dishonesty, and then the best sharper will win. What would you do if you saw a man cheating at cards? 'Bet on him!' someone has said. I visited with much interest Wall Street and the Stock Exchange, where are spent and squandered all the brains in America. For there are not many out there who think of anything but of filling their pockets. Money and money's worth you will see in abundance, but not much more. Sometimes the whole country seemed to me like a huge bank of human currency, where the bodies and souls of men were bought and sold—life being but so much to the credit-account, death creating but a momentary debit in the great ledger of a book-keeping, metallic humanity. 'Suppose, sir, that the rope should break?' asked a stranger, as he watched a car start, which was raised or lowered on an inclined plane by steam power. 'Oh, they all paid before they went,' replied the man in charge.

And, thus, the great men of society in America are simply those who have made gigantic fortunes; for money in all its multiples is the graduating index to social favour and distinction. Value in cash is the universal criterion, and the millionaires are the nobility of the land. In New England wealth has proved itself a torpedo of annihilation to the past pretensions of the *Mayflower* and its crew; while in New York the old Dutch families, 'the genuine knickerbockers,' are but nominally the *van*-guard of the social phalanx; and as for 'Chestnut' Street in Philadelphia, it is as antiquated as its name plainly indicates.

VI.

I cannot boast that I stood on every square inch of a country, the area of which is over thirty and a half million square miles. Indeed, when I think of its immense size and of the extent of our travels—from Newport on the one side to Niagara on the other, and from the shores of Lake Champlain in the north to the banks of the Potomac in the south—I feel as though I had no more than landed on that mighty continent. However, this is not so great a drawback as you might suppose, for America, I should imagine, is the easiest place in the world to see and to get to know well in a short time and within a small compass. Everything is so public, and the people are so frank and cordial—to say nothing of the inestimable and unique advantage that there is in visiting a foreign country where your own language is spoken. Nowhere can a stranger get naturalized sooner. You are heartily welcomed by Uncle Sam. You are asked to walk 'right' in by Brother Jonathan. You are immediately introduced all round. Acquaintance is instantaneous; familiarity follows soon; and friendship even may ripen within the hour. Nothing is dilatory: from trains to love, all is at full steam. So, you can see and hear everything at once. Reserve does not balk you; they put their best leg forward without any ado, and hasten to tell you their whole history from beginning to end. All their goods are in the shop window; there is nothing stowed away on a shelf and hidden from vulgar gaze. All is on the surface and open to public view. There are no shades or shadows to wonder about, or secret chambers to explore. There are no scenes to go behind. There is nothing mysterious; but all things are as bright and clear as their diaphanous atmosphere. There is, accordingly, little burrowing or sifting or close inspection required in order to gain the most complete and accurate information about everything in the country. Indeed, America seemed to me like some great show, and a peep at it is quite sufficient.

There is, too, so much advertising and labelling

and 'checking'; for at a journey's end a traveller there cannot have his pick of the luggage as he can here. In this huge hotch-potch of places and people, there is evidently a strong desire to distinguish and regulate matters wherever this can in any wise be done. And this feeling accounts, I think, for a certain remarkable and characteristic trait of Americans that may be seen in their great love of nomenclature, and in their extreme reverence for statistics, and in the general wish and anxiety for clearness and decision on all possible occasions. For instance, as to their well-known habit of addressing you by name always in conversation, I may say that I never properly realized what my own name was until I was in the States, but there I soon learnt what it was; and the lesson was so persistently taught me that I do not think that I shall ever forget it. But, seriously, there is no end to the naming, numbering, and tabulating of all things. The towns are built in square blocks, and the streets are rectangular, and the numbers of the houses continuous. Some cities are mapped out long before they are built. Washington still exists to a great extent on paper only; like a child completing a toy picture of scraps, time is gradually filling in the spaces and ratifying the original plan. Even New York City is like a head of Indian maize, each grain or section of it being regularly divided off from the rest. Amid so much that is varied and loose, the people seem to take a special delight in collecting together and classifying somehow whatever they can lay hold of. They long to get things into some shape or form, and under some heading or other. Thus, systems and schedules, statistics and calculations, and names and figures, and plans and theories, and reasons and arguments about all things are plentiful. I saw many signs of this trait.

Probably this excessive regularity and precision are, also, partly due to the fact that America had to deliberately start and set in motion, without any previous growth and preparation, all its affairs, from the form of its government down to the smallest domestic arrangements. The constitution is written; society is punctilious. Matters there did not, as in Europe, grow imperceptibly and unaccountably in the course of successive ages, and therefore in their inauguration they had to be given clear and fixed shapes and powers; and these hard and fast rules still hold good, and are in active use. The constitution, which they regard as the Koran of their civilisation, limits greatly the freedom of legislation, and is constantly preventing changes from being hurriedly and recklessly made, or 'snapped,' by any party. But in old countries, towns and constitutions, houses and streets, societies and laws, are the wayward outcome of a very gradual growth and development in the long lapse of time. And it is, I believe, because an American does not fully realize this that he so often fails to understand and appreciate the special aggravation which our social difficulties suffer from owing to their early origin and complicated past. The United Kingdom has an old and varied history, of which it is the ancient and variegated result. America was but yesterday founded on a distinct, theoretical plan, of which it is a direct and recent example.

Modern, up-to-date ideas of liberty, equality, and fraternity created the President, Senate, and Representatives. Time, custom, and tradition have found us with a King, Lords, and Commons. And for these reasons, too, written law, rigidly enforced according to the clearly-printed letter, governs there much more than common law and equity, because, as its powers have from the beginning been defined and well-known, it has always been quite apparent when it happened to fail in meeting a new want, and fresh legislation could then easily be supplied, and so there would not arise any necessity to have recourse to equitable considerations. In a young country society and legislation about keep pace, and no arrears requiring extraneous assistance accrue; but in an old country, where legislation, starting late in the day, has always lagged behind the general progress of society and the new and increasing wants of each age, custom and equity have to step in and help to make up for these delays and deficiencies.

VII.

Simple and candid, without pretence or concealment, the American people, racy of their own wide land, are free and easy in manner, speech, looks, and dress. There is no secrecy or hypocrisy about them. The Yankee seldom has his tongue in his cheek—but he may have a double quid of tobacco there; and hence, though he may make a clean breast of it, he probably will not make a similar dental display. The fact is, that there is nothing to hide or smooth over in a country where all is so rough and so plain. For everything, good or bad, is public and bare to the elbow; there is nothing up their sleeves. Nothing is done in a corner—there are no corners in this broad, open sphere, unless it be a financial one. All is above board; there is no underground. Elevated, like their unsightly railroads, in all men's eyes, the worst is at least seen and known. There are no suspicious backstairs. Their jobs are flagrant acts, not underhand schemes. The public buildings are really public, and the political leaders are not philosophic recluses. The doors of the official buildings in Washington stand wide open. No officious flunkey and pompous secretary hedge a deified minister. If you like you can slap the President on the back. Ceremonious red-tapeism and dull solemnity have departed before good-humour and common-sense.

'The administration should be conducted behind glass doors,' said Cleveland, expressing the general opinion as to the publicity that should surround the acts of public servants. There is no aggravating and unnecessary mysteriousness. Everything stands for what it is worth, and nobody can pretend. There is nothing fictitious or deceptive; they do not wink at things; there are no whisperers. They call a spade a spade, you hear nothing about 'an agricultural implement.' Their speech is direct enough; it is often slang; no grandiloquent phraseology, or wiseacre nodding and nudging about nothing, but always plain, frank words, and clear, bold acts about something.

And this remarkable publicity of political and official life in America is not, I think, sufficiently taken into account in the usual judgments and criticisms passed upon them; and many have been greatly misled by some of its effects, which they have noticed but not sought to explain. For example, the blemishes in their public life are so notorious that their comparative enormity has been much exaggerated, and they are considered exceptional, when in reality they are just as common elsewhere, though not so conspicuous; for we must never forget that in America everything, including the worst, is public. Take the hackneyed charge of political bribery. Certainly there are grounds for it. In fact, it is the avowed occupation of some. Lobbying, or corruptly influencing legislators, is an actual profession, and one which both women and men follow. But let us see how we stand in this matter. And, in the first place, we should remember that if a man or a nation is corrupt, they will be so in the direction and pursuit of their peculiar ambitions. Now the universal ambition in America is wealth. Indeed, there is no other end open to a Yankee, whatever be the career which he may choose to follow; for there is little honourable position, whether of rank or in social esteem, to be won in any line ; and this is certainly so in politics. Even the President, when his term of office is over, relapses into unhonoured private life, and no one sees or hears or cares anything more about him. On account, then, of this absence of any kind of social reward, the ambitious and not over-scrupulous politician has to find some other attraction in order to induce him to take a part in public life, and, for these reasons, he goes in for making it profitable ; and thus repays himself for his time and services. For in politics there is generally a covetous end somewhere, since there are not many in any country who are willing to be martyrs *pro bono publico*—or to work without getting some wages or recompense. Accordingly, as the American politician receives no honours or privileges, in cash-payment will be found his particular temptation—and often his price.

But do we not traffic just as much in honours and social position—the direction in which all our ambitions turn? And, in this way, have not many of our politicians their temptation—and their price, too? It may be said that cash is a grosser form of bribery, but that is only an æsthetic distinction, and all I wish to point out is that the corruption is the same, although the means may, in character and obviousness, be very different; for these in each case are determined by the nature of what is locally considered success in life. I maintain that the vote of an American politician cannot be bought with dollars a whit more easily than one in this country can with a title; and also that corruption is not less real and culpable, because less evident or vulgar. And, in what I have said, I have taken no note of the extent to which money passes between us also.

In reference to this question it is often asked: Why do not the best men in America go into politics and take their proper place in public life? But it seems to me that they do; for there do not exist any wonderful, fastidious class of saints who, if they could only be induced to come forward, would change and purify the political atmosphere. In my opinion there is not in the United States a better, brighter, or more honest body of men as a whole (of course I do not refer to a few literary and intellectual individuals, who may make the rest of the world appear very tainted beside them, since it is of the nature and very genius of such men to be retired and hidden) than the regular politicians. They are the best class of citizens that the country has produced

American Traits

up to this, and many of them are excellent and would adorn any Republic.

There is nothing, either, to prevent the other classes—the business men and millionaires—from taking part in public life but that they are, even in local and municipal matters, the worst citizens, and prefer to devote all their time and abilities to amassing wealth and adding and adding to it. Probably they are dull men as well, and I am sure that they are not honester. Good business men generally are dull, and are always greedy. The best men, then, do and have come forward—those who can take an intelligent interest in the affairs of their country and whose aims are at least to some extent patriotic and unselfish. Better classes than these are like the better newspapers in America—they do not exist.

A quite pleasing feature, however, of American political life, deserving special mention, is the absence of undue acrimony between the various parties. Although they hold their views strongly, and are, as a rule, thoroughly loyal to their platforms—every plank of them—and although on many vital questions they are very much divided, these public differences do not engender any private feelings of bitterness and animosity. No personal hatred and enmity ensue. Nor, again, does any one body of politicians seek to arrogate to itself an inherent superiority to all others. No party, for instance, would presume to appropriate exclusively the name and practice of patriotism.

Each man, of course, thinks his own opinion the right one, but they are wide-minded enough to tolerate and expect contrary opinions. They recognise that views on important and complex questions of government and legislation may, and probably always will vary. There is no intimidation; and no section dares to entitle itself the one and only true fold. The sheep are not necessarily all on one side and the goats on the other. And this spirit of toleration does not arise from indifference, from a lack of earnestness and determination, for the Yankees are not famous for holding their opinions lightly, or for yielding them easily. If the occasion is vital and demands it, there will be resolution and sturdiness enough shown. A nation that went to war with itself is not wanting in decision. But this general tolerance in their political and social life is due, I think, to the fact that, as there are no classes and hereditary distinctions, or professional or other privileges, no portion of the community can be popularly dubbed the special and traditional foe of any other. There, opinions only divide men, and all parties welcome and invite such classical differences.

VIII.

They are, too, a brave and earnest people. There is no finer or more hopeful trait than their splendid energy and pluck in all social difficulties. Never daunted or despairing, they do not allow that there is any evil, however widespread and inveterate,

American Traits

that cannot be exterminated, or at least greatly lessened. Indeed, they are seldom at a loss for a perfect cure; for in their youthful eyes no ill exists without a remedy. This new country knows not of original sin. So, they never shirk confronting the worst face to face. A failure or defeat does not dishearten them; they rely always on their inexhaustible recuperative power. They are, certainly, a grand people for rising to new emergencies and situations, however strange and dangerous they may seem; for they sincerely believe in the progress of human affairs, and act accordingly, without fear or question.

And, although this attitude may perhaps generally be too optimistic, and although it has in some remarkable instances proved so, nevertheless it is wonderful how many of our recognised and long-standing social blemishes can be at any rate mitigated, if a consciousness of their dreadful evil and appalling prevalence is brought home to all minds by an open and public manifestation of censure and disgust. It may doubtless be said that there is plenty of room for improvement; but is it not a great matter that there is a real anxiety and capacity for improvement, and an entire absence of hypocrisy? With a nation, as with an individual, are there not here the main and essential requirements of reform? And it is owing to the presence and power of this healthy spirit that they never tire of making honest attempts to deal with all the old and the fresh ills of civilization. They have a Civil Service reform party; some States have tried to put down all forms of gambling and betting; there is a strong Prohibition party; and they have made valiant efforts to purify the morals of city life. When I see all this, I understand how truly has America been described as 'the great test or trial case for all the problems and promises and speculations of humanity, and of the past and present.'. The whole country is indeed one vast experiment.

Their absolute freedom from any of the shackles of age or tradition or custom is also splendid and most refreshing. They are not in the least afraid of novelty. Far from the newness of anything being a drawback to it, the newer it is the better it is in the eyes of an American. It has never been tried before; here perhaps is the desired solution or end. They neither know nor care any more about precedents, as authorities, than ordinary folk do about a previous existence; for they understand and appreciate the 'true use of precedents,' which, in these quickly-changing days, and certainly in their growing country, is more as a warning, to show what ought to be avoided, than as a guide, to show what should be followed. In these times, what suited yesterday is, as a general rule, *ipso facto* unsuitable to-day. But in the United States all things are fearlessly tested. No word or theory or metal that ever was coined goes unassayed.

American Traits

And so they are always ready and willing to make an experiment. If that is, as has been said, the true criterion of wisdom in a man, then they are no fools; for are they not justly celebrated for their numerous new and original 'notions,' for their daring scientific discoveries, and for the countless mechanical contrivances they have with marvellous ingenuity invented? Fifty years ago Emerson said that steam was almost an Englishman. Can we not to-day say as truly that electricity is almost an American? Certainly Edison is.

One of the most remarkable and interesting institutions that I saw was the Patent Office in Washington, in which are collected exact miniature models of every kind of new machine and utensil, showing their extraordinary abilities and skill in this line, in devising infinite, infinitesimal ways of saving a hair's breadth of space, or a second of time, or a fraction of a cent—a very striking monument to their unexampled inventive genius.

IX.

But the abuses and the exaggerations of many of the good points of American life and character —the vigour and freshness, the unpretentiousness and good-humour, the equality and sociability, the frankness and independence, the freedom and tolerance, the general easiness and publicity—are also very evident. These excellent qualities have their bad sides. Frankness encourages vulgarity and impudence. Sociability can become garrulous and inquisitive and tiresome. Restless energy leads at times to impulsive and awkward action. Bold and positive speech entails much bluster and buncombe.

The independent gait which the nation cultivates looks often like an outrageous attempt to hector and swagger, and in this respect their conduct would sometimes be very serious were it not that the Yankee hardly ever means all that he says. He does not really take much to heart, and in any case will not dwell on it long. They can brag pleasantly, as when one boasts that he can dive deeper, stay down longer, and come up drier than any other man; but their humour often degenerates into mere flippancy and irreverence, and in this way there is nothing, however sacred, that has not been well vulgarized. Again, though there is something very healthy and attractive in the absence of all foolish pretence and grandeur, there are occasions when dignity and solemnity are necessary, and they are difficult to maintain without the masks of pomp and ceremony. Then enthusiasm is liable to run away into fanaticism, and eagerness means thoughtlessness and superficiality.

Freshness, also, looks like rawness, while an extravagant love of novelty and enterprise, and an enjoyment in them for their own sakes, leads at times to much rashness and folly, as is very apparent in some of their ventures and customs,

American Traits

such as horseracing in the evening by electric light. In such absurd undertakings and false developments, nature and reason are completely lost sight of, and yield place to childish artifice and whim.

Their easy tolerance of differences, also, tends to breed a certain callousness and shamelessness all round. While they do not condemn with undue severity, or make a public scapegoat of some miserable sinner, yet it must be admitted that they sometimes with culpable indifference allow notorious criminals to occupy and continue in places of public honour and trust in the government of the country. And to this the following quotation from the 'Republic' of Plato is, I think, apposite:

'Have you failed to notice in such a commonwealth,' says Socrates, in discussing a democratic form of government, 'how men who have been condemned to death or exile stay all the same, and walk about the streets, and parade like heroes, as if no one saw or cared? And is there not something splendid in the forbearance of such a commonwealth, and in its entire superiority to petty considerations? Nay, it positively scorns the doctrine which, when we were founding our State, we laid down with an air of importance, to the effect that no one who is not endowed with an extraordinary nature can ever become a good man, unless from his earliest childhood he plays among beautiful objects, and studies all beautiful things.

How magnificently it tramples all this underfoot, without troubling itself in the least about the previous pursuits of those who enter on a political course, whom it raises to honour, if they only assert that they wish well to the commons.'

Again, open-to-the-public applying almost indiscriminately to everything has its disadvantages. Private life becomes a practical impossibility. Manners, also, are demonstrative. Every *tête-à-tête* is a public address; for a round table is the least an American will ever confer with. Thus every conversation is an interview, and any casual remark is treated as an official announcement, and the most private family details become matters of newspaper gossip. Indeed, nowhere is the bad effect of this unrestricted publicity seen more glaringly than in American journalism, which no words of mine could sufficiently stigmatise as totally wanting in taste, whether literary, social, or moral.

Journalism in the States is for the most part the following of common eavesdroppers and scandal-scavengers. A certain class of newspaper correspondents are simply domestic spies, who pry into the precincts of boudoirs and parlours, and filch the secrets of escritoires and blotting-pads. What news they have has been overheard or stolen. A keyhole is their principal point of view. On bended knees they scrape together what unfiltered family filth they can detect. Most of their reports come from behind curtains and screens, and consist of the bickerings and misfortunes of some unhappy fireside. The adventures recorded and fully described are generally movements 'from the blue bed to the brown,' not quite so innocent as those of the worthy Vicar of Wakefield and his faithful spouse. The language and style of composition, also, form a complete grammar and glossary of the latest slang, and in vulgarity, scurrility, and indecency emulate the unfortunate beings who infest the lowest purlieus of the Bowery. Their statements, too, are usually made recklessly and falsely. Even the best journals are a daily libel on every body and thing. Actions are not taken against them for the simple reason that it is impossible to indict a whole profession.

Thus their numerous sheets and columns are filled nearly exclusively with accounts of the most demoralising and wretched practices of mankind. The less worthy the actor or the event, the more attention it receives from the American press. If you want notoriety cheaply, go and behave infamously in the States. Of course, this publicity, by bringing public opinion to bear on matters and so helping to put an end to them, may sometimes be beneficial to society; but is such conspicuous notice necessary for that end? or is not all this minute research into and public disclosure —twice daily, Sundays not excepted—of the pestilential doings of such insignificant and miserable creatures a disgraceful pandering on the part of a noble profession to the weakness and pruriency of human nature?

The Americans have, in fine, all the good and bad traits of a young and enthusiastic people. Indeed, in many ways, they struck me as being even a childish people: rapturously delighted with any trifle or bauble, and foolishly chagrined at any little disappointment or check, yet always quickly recovering from either sensation, and passing obliviously on to some new entertainment; inordinately proud of their possessions and achievements, while ludicrously sensitive under any adverse criticism. When you land the first question which will immediately be put to you will be, 'Well, sir, and what do you think of our country?' It is said that a Yankee has been known to have asked this question of a stranger even at sea when the land was only in sight. But, early or late, you must never forget that there is only one answer which will satisfy them, and that is the clear and unqualified response, 'I guess your country is the finest in the world.' And in so speaking you will be but complying with a necessity which, for social success and good-will, is absolutely essential on all occasions. I knew that I should be expected to like most of their things, but I had not realized that I should have to praise in extravagant and indecorous terms everything in the country. But they are morbidly sensitive of the opinions of strangers, and cannot endure any impression that is not entirely favourable. Without experience you cannot conceive how touchy and huffy they are in this respect, and how strongly they resent any passing word that is not expressive of envious admiration of them and all their ways and customs. Their own dignity and self-respect—if they exist—seem to be of no avail. And they are most suspicious of your favourable opinion even, unless you couch it in language which we should consider lavish and fulsome, if not in positively bad taste. But no key is too high for them. I remember on one occasion a lady showing us some new wall-paper that she had just put up in her house. I said that I thought it 'very pretty,' but when I heard an American gentleman who was present pronounce it 'perfectly exquisite!' I felt that I had not reached the proper note, and that I had perhaps, though quite innocently, damned it, in her eyes, with faint praise. For they understand nothing but gross adulation and flattery, and criticism or discrimination, however slight and superficial, is invariably regarded as rude and unwarrantable. And yet these same people are captiously critical of us.

They are, indeed, a young people—a nation of emancipated children. But how promising! The good heart and disposition and the bright mind are there, and time will bring what is lacking in weight and judgment, and in dignity and repose. Doubtless they will grow wiser as they grow older.

X.

In conclusion, then, the Americans are a quick, bold, emphatic people. Bright and brisk, they hit a nail on the head—bang! No beating about the bush, even in play. Baseball is a rough, hard-hitting game. Far and wide though the land is, they are always on the spot, and a determined Yankee is a tough customer. You cannot easily surprise or thwart him. He will carry out his idea, even at the expense of a civil war. When the occasion has demanded it, they have had recourse to Coercion Acts, which they call Force Bills, and they have administered them rigorously. The President is chosen on the most popular of franchises, but when elected he is the greatest of autocrats.

Again, the unfailing life and enterprise, and the unwavering pluck and faith of this fresh, enthusiastic, self-reliant people—seriously endeavouring to cope with the many difficult problems of social and economic life, and firmly believing in the possible improvement, and even in the ultimate perfection of the human race—are very attractive. Brave and earnest, they manfully take the bull by the horns, and never admit of any dilemmas. The whole community is one great committee of ways and means, and the country is clearly determined to rely always on its own resources, as the protective tariff and the general air of independence demonstrate.

Superior souls do not, perhaps, grow in abundance in the States any more than they do elsewhere, since they are rare flowers in all soils. But, leaving them out of consideration, you will find a host of active, hearty, generous, intelligent people, taking all things in good-humour, for there is much unaffected simplicity and friendliness, and geniality, and common humaneness and charity among them. The heart is always there, and always true, and intelligence is never wanting either; but the intellect and soul are not so evident or real. Even the beacon light of Boston has now completely gone out, and only the faintest twilight of its past 'transcendental' brilliancy remains. 'The last leaf on the bough' gently dropped to earth a couple of autumns ago, and winter and darkness have set in.

But, after all, the main fact about America is not yet to be seen, for it is the distant future. On nothing does it rely so much. It hardly claims, so far, to be more than a land of promise—and its practice admittedly does not come up to its preaching. Its ideals—and no country is more idealistic—are very far ahead of the realities. So that, to appreciate or understand the true meaning and force of the nation, one should be more a student of the future than of the present or the past. One's philosophy should be prophetic rather than historical, and rest more on what man may yet be and do than on what he has already been and done.

One often hears it said that there are no ideas in America, but in one important way that is a great mistake; for American political and social life, unlike that of other countries, where it is the vulgar outcome of a long chain of fortuitous circumstances, is based on an idea, and is deeply influenced by this origin. Theoretical conception is the foundation and guiding principle of the nation as a democracy, and of the government as a republic.

An ideal Utopia is ever before the eyes of the people, and is the vitalizing incentive of all their hopes, and wishes, and actions. Although it may not have appeared in any very tangible or practical shape, nevertheless, their glowing trust in the future, and in its rich possibilities, and their high aspirations as a commonwealth, are clear signs and proofs of its real presence and strength. Beneath all their bad there is the idea of good, and that is a great trait. They firmly believe that everything is tending, however slowly and waywardly, towards the ultimate realization of an almost perfect state of affairs, and they strive and work with that great end in view. It is, in fact, only their strong and unshaken belief in it that has enabled the country to survive and surmount such a trial as the Civil War, and that has kept the Government going, in spite of the many unexampled difficulties which it has had to encounter.

But their faith in the future of the States, and in the inherent perfectibility of the people is absolute. America has been well described as the 'type of progress and of essential faith in man above all his errors and wickedness.' 'The land of liberty, and the asylum of the oppressed,' it stands before the world to justify the wisdom and power of trusting in common humanity. Blemishes are but passing and indispensable signs of growth.

American Traits

And so they look to the end more than to the means, and are willing—perhaps too much so—to forgive and forget the present in their love and admiration of the future. For, in their eyes the tide of social evolution is true, though every wave ring false. The goal of political progress is right, though every move seem wrong. The whole is good, though all its parts confound one. Whatever, therefore, the country may be in practice and reality, it is most ideal in theory and aim. American democracy is not merely a fact—vulgar and base, perhaps, according to the fastidious tastes of some—but it is also a great and noble idea, and one ever-present in the minds and hearts of the people.

But the country is young. It is not yet out of its teens. It is still growing, and is not therefore really fit for presentation. Like its great poet, the nation says:

'Not to-day is to justify me and answer what I am for;
But you, a new brood, native, athletic, continental, greater than before known,
Arouse! for you must justify me!'

For the American people believe that they have a great future before them, and not behind them, as is so much the feeling here. They have all the superb strength of youth, rich in the adolescent powers of unspent virility, and have not to be content with the feeble efforts of senility, lame and exhausted, and depending on the artificial substitutes, experience, habit, and memory. They are primarily believers in things, not as they were, or as they are, but as they yet will be. Life is not a foregone conclusion, but it is an unknown quantity —mysterious, incalculable, magnificent. So you need make no appeal on the score of the past; they care nothing about it; it does not impress or overpower them. They would break all records; bygones are bygones. They do not live on memories of the past, but on anticipations of the future, and they confidently point to it in exculpation of everything in the present. It is their real pride and glory. They already boast of posterity and its works, and even claim to be themselves reflectively ennobled and transfigured by the blood of future generations, and by the splendour and renown of the brave days to come.

Accordingly, while our outlook is gloomy, theirs is always radiant. However bad the signs of the times, or dark the shadows of coming events, happy and trustful they see the light of the future beyond; for they have all the glorious hope and life and freshness of a dawn desirous of fulfilling a day. And how refreshing and invigorating this faith and self-reliance and optimism are! And how timid and despondent must we not seem to them! For, while we think the present bad enough, and, rightly or wrongly, appear to dread the future, they, on the contrary, eagerly hail and welcome it, trusting devoutly in its healing and perfecting powers, since, whatever may be thought of the past or of the present state of affairs, they have an invincible belief in the providential destiny of their great republic.

www.ingramcontent.com/pod-product-compliance
Lightning Source LLC
Chambersburg PA
CBHW031344160426
43196CB00007B/732